The Indian Wars

Books in the America's Wars Series:

The Indian Wars

by Don Nardo

America's WARS

Lucent Books, P.O. Box 289011, San Diego, CA 92198-0011

Library of Congress Cataloging-in-Publication Data

Nardo, Don, 1947-
     The Indian wars / by Don Nardo.
         p.   cm. — (America's wars)
     Includes bibliographical references and index.
     Summary: A discussion of the hostilities between European-American settlers and the native American population and their impact on both settlers and Indians.
     ISBN 1-56006-403-X
     1. Indians of North America—Wars—Juvenile literature.
[1. Indians of North America—Wars.] I. Title. II. Series.
E81.N67   1991
973—dc20   91-23068
                                           CIP
                                         AC

Copyright 1991 by Lucent Books, Inc., P.O. Box 289011,
San Diego, CA 92198-0011

Contents

Foreword

War, justifiable or not, is a descent into madness. George Washington, America's first president and commander-in-chief of its armed forces, wrote that his most fervent wish was "to see this plague of mankind, war, banished from the earth." Most, if not all of the forty presidents who succeeded Washington have echoed similar sentiments. Despite this, not one generation of Americans since the founding of the republic has been spared the maelstrom of war. In its brief history of just over two hundred years, the United States has been a combatant in eleven major wars. And four of those conflicts have occurred in the last fifty years.

America's reasons for going to war have differed little from those of most nations. Political, social, and economic forces were at work which either singly or in combination ushered America into each of its wars. A desire for independence motivated the Revolutionary War. The fear of annihilation led to the War of 1812. A related fear, that of having the nation divided, precipitated the Civil War. The need to contain an aggressor nation brought the United States into the Korean War. And territorial ambition lay behind the Mexican-American and the Indian Wars. Like all countries, America, at different times in its history, has been victimized by these forces and its citizens have been called to arms.

Whatever reasons may have been given to justify the use of military force, not all of America's wars have been popular. From the Revolutionary War to the Vietnam War, support of the people has alternately waxed and waned. For example, less than half of the colonists backed America's war of independence. In fact, most historians agree that at least one-third were committed to maintaining America's colonial status. During the Spanish-American War, a strong antiwar movement also developed. Resistance to the war was so high that the Democratic party made condemning the war a significant part of its platform in an attempt to lure voters into voting Democratic. The platform stated that "the burning issue of imperialism growing out of the Spanish war involves the very existence of the Republic and the destruction of our free institutions." More recently, the Vietnam War divided the nation like no other conflict had since the Civil War. The mushrooming antiwar movements in most major cities and colleges throughout the United States did more to bring that war to a conclusion than did actions on the battlefield.

Yet, there have been wars which have enjoyed overwhelming public support. World Wars I and II were popular because people believed that the survival of America's democratic institutions was at stake. In both wars, the American people rallied with an enthusiasm and spirit of self-sacrifice that was remarkable for a country with such a diverse population. Support for food and fuel rationing, the purchase of war bonds, a high rate of voluntary enlistments, and countless other forms of voluntarism, were characteristic of the people's response to those wars. Most recently, the Persian Gulf War prompted an unprecedented show of support even though the United States was not directly threatened by the conflict. Rallies in support of U.S. troops were widespread. Tens of thousands of individuals, including families, friends, and well-wishers of the troops sent packages of food, cosmetics, clothes, cassettes, and suntan oil. And even more supporters wrote letters to unknown soldiers that were forwarded to the military front. In fact, most public opinion polls revealed that up to 90 percent of all Americans approved of their nation's involvement.

The complex interplay of events and purposes that leads to military conflict should be included in a history of any war. A simple chronicling of battles and casualty lists at best offers only a partial history of war. Wars do not spontaneously erupt; nor does their memory perish. They are driven by underlying causes, fueled by policymakers, fought and supported by citizens, and remembered by those plotting a nation's future. For these reasons wars, or the fear of wars, will always leave an indelible stamp on any nation's history and influence its future.

The purpose of this series is to provide a full understanding of America's wars by presenting each war in a historical context. Each of the twelve volumes focuses on the events that led up to the war, the war itself, its impact on the home front, and its aftermath and influence upon future conflicts. The unique personalities, the dramatic acts of courage and compassion, as well as the despair and horror of war are all presented in this series. Together, they show why America's wars have dominated American consciousness in the past as well as how they guide many political decisions of today. In these vivid and objective accounts, students will gain an understanding of why America became involved in these conflicts, and how historians, military and government officials, and others have come to understand and interpret that involvement.

Chronology of Events

1607
John Smith establishes first permanent English settlement in North America at Jamestown, Virginia, with extensive contact with the Powhatan Confederacy.

1621
Pilgrims make peace with Chief Massasoit of the Wampanoags, the first treaty between whites and Indians. They celebrate the peace and bountiful harvest with the first Thanksgiving.

1626
Canarsee Indians sell Manhattan Island, which belongs to Manhattan Indians, to governor of New Netherlands for trade goods.

1636–1637
Pequot war in New England; Colonists kill more than 600 men, women, and children in a surprise attack on stockaded Pequot village.

1675–1676
King Philip's War; Metacomet killed.

1680
Pueblo Indians under Popé drive Spanish out of their area.

1763
Treaty of Paris ends French and Indian War; King George III proclaims Appalachian Mountains as end of British settlement, establishing protected Indian Country west of the mountains; Pontiac's rebellion begins against the British in the Great Lakes region.

1774
Virginia settlers and Shawnees fight Lord Dunsmore's War.

1787
Northwest Ordinance calls for reservations, Indian rights, and guidelines for developing Old Northwest Territory.

1789
U.S. Constitution ratified.

1790–1794
Little Turtle's War begins in Old Northwest; Battle of Fallen Timbers.

1804
Louisiana Territory Act vows to move eastern Indians west of the Mississippi.

1809
Under Treaty of Fort Wayne, Gen. William Henry Harrison gets 1.5 million acres of Indian land in Ohio and Indiana.

1809–1811
Tecumseh's rebellion; Tenskwatawa is defeated at Tippecanoe.

1813
Tecumseh killed fighting for British in War of 1812.

1814
In Treaty of Fort Jackson, Andrew Jackson takes land from Creeks.

1817
Andrew Jackson invades Florida in Seminole War.

1819
Spain cedes Florida to United States.

1824
Bureau of Indian Affairs created within War Department.

1825
Indian Country west of Mississippi defined.

1827
Cherokees adopt a constitution patterned upon that of the United States, but Georgia legislature voids it.

1830
Congress passes the Indian Removal Act relocating eastern Indians west of the Mississippi.

1831–1839
Five civilized tribes of southeast are relocated to Indian territory.

1832
Black Hawk War begins with Sauk and Fox Indians against the United States in Wisconsin and Illinois.

1838
Osceola dies in prison during Second Seminole War.

1838–1839

Cherokee "trail of tears."

1846

England cedes Oregon country to the United States.

1847

Cayuse Indian War begins in Oregon.

1851

Treaty of Laramie between whites and tribes of northern plains.

1853–1856

United States acquires 174 million acres of Indian lands through 52 treaties, all of which whites eventually break.

1860

Paiute War (or Pyramid Lake War) in Nevada.

1861

U.S. Civil War begins.

1861–1863

Chiefs Cochise and Mangas Coloradas lead Apache uprisings in Southwest after the Bascom affair.

1862

Santee Sioux under Chief Little Crow lead uprising in Minnesota.

1862

Thirty-eight Sioux hanged in Mankato for uprising.

1863–1866

Navajo War in New Mexico and Arizona ends; Navajos are forced to make the Long Walk to Bosque Redondo.

1864–1865

Cheyenne-Arapaho War in Colorado and Kansas.

1864

Chivington's Colorado volunteers massacre more than 300 Indians at Sand Creek.

1865

With the end of the Civil War, "Five Civilized Tribes" are punished for supporting the south by losing half of Indian Territory to twenty other tribes from Kansas and Nebraska.

1866

Railroad Enabling Act allows railroads to take Indian lands for construction.

1866–1868

War for Bozeman Trail in Wyoming and Montana.

1867

Hancock campaign against Cheyennes and Arapahos on central plains.

1867

Medicine Lodge Treaty promises permanent Indian lands in Indian Territory.

1867

Peace Commission recommends end of treaty process and negotiates the last Indian treaty with the Nez Percé.

1868

Second Fort Laramie Treaty ends conflict over the Bozeman Trail.

1868

Indians are denied the right to vote under the 14th Amendment.

1868–1869

Southern Plains War (Sheridan Campaign) against Cheyennes, Sioux, Arapahos, Kiowas, and Comanches.

1871

General Sheridan orders Indians to remain on reservations until civilian agent gives them permission to leave.

1871

Congress prohibits the signing of Indian treaties.

1872–1873

Modoc War in California and Oregon; Modoc leader Captain Jack hanged.

1874

Custer's expedition into the Black Hills discovers gold.

1874–1875

Quanah Parker leads Comanches, Kiowas, and Cheyennes in Red River War on southern plains.

1876
Custer defeated at Little Bighorn.

1877
Flight of Nez Percé under Chief Joseph in northwest.

1877–1880
Victorio leads Apache resistance in southwest.

1878
Bannock War in Idaho and Oregon.

In this fanciful illustration, Gen. Armstrong Custer rides out in a last charge at Little Bighorn.

1879
Ute War in Colorado.

1879
Federal court at Omaha, Nebraska, rules that Standing Bear is a person under the law.

1881
Sitting Bull and his band of 187 surrender at Fort Buford, North Dakota.

1881–1886
Geronimo leads Apache resistance in the Southwest.

1885
Last great herd of buffalo exterminated.

1886
Geronimo surrenders.

1887
Congress passes the General Allotment Act (the Dawes Act), which divides reservation land into individually owned parcels and takes extra land.

1890
Ghost Dance movement led by a Paiute prophet spreads a Christianlike religion among northern Plains tribes.

1890
Sitting Bull killed on Standing Rock Reservation.

1890
Massacre at Wounded Knee virtually wipes out Big Foot's band of Miniconjou Sioux.

1901
Snake uprising in Oklahoma Territory in which Creek Indians resist allotment.

1906
U.S. government takes 50,000 acres of sacred Taos Pueblo land in the Blue Lake region of New Mexico and makes it a national park.

1924
Citizenship Act grants U.S. citizenship to all native-born Indians.

1928
Charles Curtis, a Kaw Indian and U.S. senator, is elected vice president of the United States under President Herbert Hoover.

1928
After two years of study, the Meriam Report declares the allotment system a failure.

1930
Northern Cheyenne Reservation becomes last communally owned reservation to be alloted.

The slaughter of the buffalo by frontiersmen aboard the Kansas Pacific Railroad. By killing off the buffalo, whites effectively killed off Plains Indian tribes' traditional way of life.

1934

Indian Reorganization Act reverses the allotment policy and provides for tribal ownership and self-government.

1946

Congress creates the Indian Claims Commission to settle tribal land claims against the United States and to provide financial compensation.

1948

Arizona forced to give Indians the right to vote after trial brought by a Tewa Indian.

1961

Interior Department allows Indian tribes the first chance to purchase lands offered for sale by individual Indians.

1968

Project Own launched by Small Business Administration guaranteeing loans to help Indians open small businesses on reservations.

1972

Trail of Broken Treaties Caravan marches on Washington to demonstrate on behalf of injustices.

1973

Congress returns federal services under Menominee Restoration Act, reverses termination policy.

1978

Indian Claims Commission ends after granting $800 million to tribes over the years.

1980

Maine Indian Claims Settlement Act creates federal land acquisition fund for Passamaquoddy and Penobscot Indians.

1983

President Reagan vetoes a $900,000 congressional land-claim suit brought by Pequot tribe against the state of Connecticut.

INTRODUCTION

Wars of Resistance

The British, French, and other Europeans began colonizing and settling the eastern coast of North America in the early 1600s. As they did so, they came into contact with Native Americans, people who had inhabited North and South America for many thousands of years. At first, these contacts were peaceful. As almost every American can relate, Indian generosity saved the Pilgrims at Plymouth, Massachusetts, and this is commemorated each year in the celebration of the first Thanksgiving. But, as white populations grew and required more and more land,

These two photos from the Carlisle School show a Navajo Indian before and after "civilization." Whites often looked upon Indians as savages who had to be reeducated to adopt civilized ways.

these contacts became increasingly violent. Much of the violence stemmed from colonists' firm stereotypes and intolerance. Early colonists thought of Indians as an impediment to peaceful white expansion. They thought of Indian resistance to white takeover as bloodthirsty violence. In turn, settlers viewed frontier families, soldiers, and cowboys as heroes, valiantly taming a hostile land and hostile people.

These stereotypes eventually developed into the theory of Manifest Destiny—the idea that whites were destined to control North America from the Atlantic to the Pacific oceans. This faith was supported, whites believed, by their obvious cultural and religious superiority over the Indians. Whites believed Indians used the land in a primitive, unsophisticated way. Indians could not really be thought to own or lay claim to land they merely hunted on and roamed over. Whites, on the other hand, would use the land. They would build farms and cities on it and bring progress and civilization with them. In addition to this belief, whites viewed their religion as clearly superior and yet another reason why they should triumph over the Indians. Indian religion seemed childish to the whites. In their eyes, a land of Christian believers seemed ultimately more progressive and more pleasing to God than the thousands of heathen hordes that populated North America.

Indians retreat from advancing white soldiers in this etching entitled "Last of the Redskins." Indians saw skirmishes with white populations as defensive; whites viewed Indians who resisted as "hostile."

Indians attack a white settlement. As more whites moved into their territory, Indians began to oppose them in greater numbers.

To the Indians, of course, none of these beliefs were compelling. As whites destroyed their villages and took over and destroyed the shape and lay of the land, Indians began to oppose the whites. Indians saw their role in clashes with whites as protecting their people, their livelihoods, culture, and traditional way of life. Some Indians attempted to live in peaceful coexistence with whites. But even when Indians would agree, through treaty, to move their villages or sell the rights to certain lands in exchange for payments or goods, whites often violated the treaties or disowned them.

Ultimately, it was this unceasing white expansion and Indian resistance to it that led to the over four hundred years of conflicts called the Indian Wars. During these conflicts, the American goal became the complete conquest of North America. One U.S. administration after another pursued this goal and fought the Indian tribes who attempted to defend their homelands and ways of life. Although the United States did not formally declare war on the Indians, its goal of conquest clearly could not allow the two civilizations to live together peacefully. Between 1780 and 1890, Americans killed hundreds of thousands of Indians and destroyed tribe after tribe. Today, we view the destruction of these cultures with a sense of grievous loss. We view the white conquest with a sense of outrage.

In the end, the Indians lost the fight to defend their homeland. But they did not lose it because of lack of bravery, skill, or

An Indian camp near Pine Ridge, South Dakota, in 1891.

sense of purpose. They simply could not oppose the overwhelming numbers of whites, streaming in from Europe. They were also defeated by a lack of unity. For most Indians, tribal identity was far more important than racial identity. This loyalty to their specific tribe left Indians at a distinct disadvantage. Whites did have a strong racial identity. No matter what disagreements they had between them, whites fought alongside one another because they shared a racial destiny. And even though several unique Indian individuals attempted to inspire the many Indian tribes to form such a union, the attempts were largely unsuccessful.

Today, the Indian Wars seem brutal, cruel, and in many cases, senseless. Many Americans cannot help but view them in the same way Carl Waldman expresses in *Atlas of the North American Indian:* "Given all that Indian culture and philosophy have to offer modern humanity—especially in terms of an ecological world view—many perhaps would like to rewrite history with the Indians having a greater hold on human destiny."

CHAPTER ONE

A Pattern of Greed and Violence

At first, Indians and newly arrived colonists from Europe got along well. It was only as colonists continued to arrive in huge numbers that clashes between settlers and Indians began.

Beginning in the early 1600s, for nearly three centuries white settlers and soldiers fought various Indian tribes for possession of North American lands. The first whites were mainly from Britain and established colonies along the east coast of the continent. These colonies rapidly expanded, and conflicts arose with the Indians who inhabited coastal areas.

British Settlers Arrive

At first, there were few troubles between whites and Indians. In fact, the Indians welcomed and helped many of the original white settlers. The first permanent British settlement was established in 1607 at Jamestown on Chesapeake Bay in Virginia. The colony started with 900 people, but the first winters were harsh, and starvation and disease killed some 750 of the colonists. The local Indians, members of the Algonquin confederacy of two hundred villages and thirty-two tribes, observed the whites' plight. The leader of the Algonquins, Wahunsenacawh, whom the colonists called Powhatan, ordered his people to give the colonists food. For a few short years, the Algonquins and colonists lived together in peace. The Indians shared their knowledge of the land with the settlers, teaching them to grow tobacco.

Eventually, tensions arose between the Indians and the inhabitants of Jamestown. Disputes occurred over control of the Indian lands near the colony. The Virginia colonists shipped their tobacco to Europe, where the market for the crop grew quickly. The colonists began taking over Indian lands to grow more tobacco. Without asking permission of the Indians, white farmers chopped down trees and planted tobacco in areas where the Indians had hunted and fished for centuries.

The colonists believed they had a right to take these lands because they were more civilized than the Indians. Although they had appreciated the Indians' earlier aid, the colonists had never considered the Indians their equals. In fact, the whites saw the Indians as wild savages who had few or no rights to the land. One British colonist described the east coast of America as "a hideous and desolate wilderness full of wild beasts and wild men." Racism was an aspect of this superior attitude. The white colonists saw the bronze-colored skin of North American Indians as a badge of inferiority.

Religious beliefs also played an important role in anti-Indian prejudice. The whites were Christians, with strong beliefs in the Bible and the existence of one all-powerful God. They were convinced that theirs was the only true faith and therefore superior to other religious ideas. They looked upon Indian beliefs in nature gods and spirits as primitive and childish. A minister who came to Virginia in the early 1600s declared that the Indians lived in a "miserable, Godless state of sin." They were "poor,

(Below) Powhatan, the leader of the Algonquin tribe, fed the first colonists, helping them to survive the winter. (Bottom) A Christian minister attempts to convert a group of Indians.

French Explorers

The first contact between French explorers and Indians occurred in 1534. In that year, Jacques Cartier sailed down the St. Lawrence River in what is now southern Canada. Like Columbus, Cartier was looking for a route to China for trade in spices.

Cartier first saw Indians from a distance, catching only glimpses of "wild and savage folk" dressed in furs, painted with tan colors, and adorned with feathers. Later, some Micmacs appeared in nine canoes carrying furs to trade. So much trade was conducted on that first day that some Indians went home naked after trading the furs off their backs. Soon, the French developed an extensive fur trade with the local Indians.

Samuel de Champlain became the first French explorer to enter what is now the United States. For a decade beginning in 1603, Champlain explored the New England coast, the Great Lakes, and New York. In 1609, he met a band of about three hundred Hurons, Algonquins, and Montagnais and helped them in their war against the Iroquois. The Iroquois remembered this episode with bitterness and later eagerly supported the British against the French.

brutish barbarians," he said, who were "not many degrees above beasts." The colonists, on the other hand, were "born and bred among civilized and Christian nations." The whites thought it was their duty to God to convert the "heathen," or ungodly, Indians to Christianity and also to control their lands. Some of the colonists used a passage from the Bible to support this belief. This passage, from the Book of Psalms, reads: "God will give him [the Christian] the heathen [to convert and watch over], and the uttermost parts of the earth for his possession." The colonists, therefore, felt that taking possession of Indian lands was moral and justified by God.

The First Indian War

After their land had been stolen, some Algonquin leaders wanted to retaliate by attacking the whites. But Chief Powhatan wanted to maintain peace and convinced his people not to retaliate. He believed that future trade with the whites would be good for the Indians. Powhatan also thought that the colonists would never need more than a few thousand extra acres. He did not think that this much land was worth fighting over and suggested that the whites could obtain the land through friendship or trade. He asked the colonists, "Why should you take by force from us that which you can obtain by love?" Although some tensions continued, Powhatan managed to maintain the peace between Indians and whites until his death in 1618.

Only four years later, the first full-scale war between Indians and whites began. Following Powhatan's death, the Jamestown colony continued to expand into Indian lands. With Powhatan gone, Algonquins who had argued for war won the support of their people. The most important of these leaders was Opechancanough, Powhatan's brother. In the spring of 1622, Opechancanough led an attack on several outlying settlements of Jamestown. At the time, the population of the colony was about fifteen hundred. In only a few hours, the Indians killed about 350 colonists and burned several dozen houses.

The reaction of the colonists was immediate and harsh. They swore to annihilate the local Algonquin tribes. The whites launched three expeditions against the Indians each year for many years. In each raid, the colonists burned Indian villages and crops and massacred all the Indians they found, including women and children. The Jamestown leaders ordered the captains of these expeditions not to give the Indians a chance to replant corn or rebuild their villages. The captains were also under orders not to make peace under any conditions. Sometimes, the colonists pretended they wanted peace and persuaded groups of Indians to return to their villages. The whites then trapped and slaughtered them.

Eventually, after more than twenty years of fighting, the colonists captured and shot Opechancanough. By this time, there were only about a thousand local Algonquins left. The colonists negotiated a treaty with the surviving Indians, establishing official boundaries separating white and Indian lands. According to the treaty, the colonists controlled all the lands along the Atlantic coast, while the Indians had to live on small pieces of land allotted by the whites. These were the first Indian reservations.

Indians and Whites Clash in New England

Although peace was established in Virginia, fighting erupted between Indians and settlers in New England, the British colonies of Massachusetts, Rhode Island, and Connecticut, a few years later. Members of the Wampanoag tribe had been slowly

Indians massacre white settlers in Virginia. Angered over white takeover of their traditional lands, Indians tried to annihilate settlers in Virginia. Whites retaliated immediately and harshly, eventually winning the conflict and signing a treaty with the few surviving Indians in the area.

Men gather their rifles in preparation for an Indian attack by Metacomet's forces.

pushed off their land and forced to live in smaller and smaller areas. A main cause of the New England war was the economic dependency of Indians on whites. As happened in other areas of North America, white settlers introduced guns to the Indians, who immediately found the weapons more efficient for hunting and fighting than bows and arrows. But the Indians became dependent on the whites for ammunition. Often, the Indians went into debt to whites. In New England, the settlers' laws demanded that people pay off their debts by working in the towns. Building fences, cleaning stables, and loading wagons were common jobs done to pay debts. Indians who did these jobs, however, often endured insults and humiliation from whites.

In 1675, a young Wampanoag leader named Metacomet grew tired of whites taking Indian land and harassing Indians trying to work off their debts. Metacomet, whom the settlers called King Philip, organized an alliance of the Wampanoag, Nipmuc, and Narraganset tribes against the whites. Small bands of Indians began attacking British settlements from the Atlantic coast of Massachusetts to the Connecticut River more than one hundred

Militia shoot at Wampanoag Indians during King Philip's War. With their superior numbers and weaponry, whites were able to defeat the Wampanoag and shatter their alliance.

Indians and colonists confront one another during King Philip's War.

miles inland. The New England colonies united and fought back in what became known as King Philip's War.

The first major battle of the war occurred on July 15, 1675, at Pocasset Swamp near Plymouth, Massachusetts. There, the colonists tried to trap Metacomet and his warriors in a marsh. Both whites and Indians became exhausted fighting in water that was often waist deep. Several dozen Indians and colonists died by gunfire, knife wounds, or drowning. Some fighters shielded themselves from attack by hiding behind floating bodies. Eventually, the tide of battle turned in favor of the colonists, who had the advantage of many more men and guns. Metacomet and the remainder of his forces managed to escape on floating rafts to the nearby Taunton River.

The fighting continued until August 1676, when Metacomet died in battle near Mount Hope, Rhode Island. By that time, the situation for the Indians of the region had become hopeless. As a result of dozens of raids and attacks by whites, Metacomet's alliance had crumbled. A majority of the Indian villages had been destroyed. The Narragansets suffered the most, losing all but one hundred of an estimated four thousand warriors. Although the colonists won the war, they too suffered heavy losses: more than seven hundred dead, thirteen towns completely burned, and six hundred homes destroyed.

The colonists' losses in the war caused strong anti-Indian sentiments among the white New Englanders. The colonists forced some of the surviving Wampanoags to live on reservations. These were usually small farming communities supervised closely by white overseers. Indians in these communities had to convert to Christianity and adopt other white customs. The colonists sold many other Wampanoags into slavery to Spanish colonies in the Caribbean Sea. This was a common practice at the time. Because of racial, religious, and other prejudices, the whites saw the defeated Indians more as spoils of war than as human beings. So, the colonists felt they had the right to sell the Indians as they pleased.

New England colonists extended their anti-Indian hatreds to other New England tribes that had been on friendly terms with whites. The Mohegans and Pequots, traditional enemies of the Wampanoags, had helped the colonists defeat Metacomet's forces. But the angry and bitter whites turned even on their Indian allies. Colonists from Massachusetts and Rhode Island forced hundreds of Pequots off of their traditional hunting grounds. The whites threatened to destroy Mohegan villages, too, if the Indians

In the French and Indian Wars, both the British and the French enlisted the aid of Indian allies. Here, Indian allies of the French defeat the British in 1755.

did not give up large tracts of land. Thus, King Philip's War set a pattern that would be repeated many times in later relations between Indians and whites in America. Whites, angry over resistance from any Indians, would punish all Indians for the actions of a few.

Indians and Whites Fighting Together

Like the New England settlers, later whites enlisted the aid of Indian allies. This practice was an important factor in the French and Indian War, the last major conflict between whites and Indians before the birth of the United States. By the mid-1700s, most of eastern North America was claimed by either the British or the French. The British ruled the colonies along the Atlantic coast east of the Appalachian Mountains. The French controlled Canada, the Great Lakes region surrounding Lakes Erie and Ontario, and parts of the Ohio Valley south of these lakes. The French goal in the war was to stop British settlers from moving westward from the Appalachian Mountains and into the Ohio Valley. The British wanted to take Canada and the Ohio Valley from the French. Each side enlisted Indians to support its cause.

Such alliances were not new to most Indians. They were used to forming alliances with other tribes to fight a common enemy. Usually, once the enemy had been defeated, the victors remained allies and maintained strong ties of mutual aid and respect. The Indians who helped the British and the French expected the same consideration from their white allies. The Indians fought in the war because they believed the whites they helped would later protect Indian hunting grounds. The Indians also fought in return for food, guns, and money. Thus, tribes of the Ohio Valley and southern Canada, like the Ottawa under Chief Pontiac, eagerly helped the French. Fighting on the British side were various tribes of the New England region, especially the powerful Iroquois. By 1763, the British and their Indian allies managed to defeat the French, and the British took complete possession of Canada. The British now controlled all former Indian lands east of the Appalachians and directly north of the Great Lakes.

Boundaries Created and Ignored

For the Indians, the most important outcome of the French and Indian War was the Proclamation Line of 1763. This was a north-south boundary line that the victorious British drew through the Appalachian Mountains. The purpose of the line was to separate Indian lands from colonial settlements and

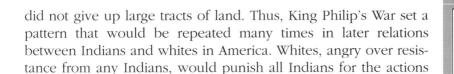

Pontiac's Resistance

Pontiac led one of the largest uprisings against British colonial advance into the Ohio Valley. He first became popular as a leader in the 1760s when he helped the French by opposing the opening of frontier lands to British settlers. In 1762, Pontiac united nearly all the tribes along the Appalachian Mountains and convinced them to attack British forts and destroy frontier settlements.

In 1763, Pontiac led a surprise raid on the British-held Fort Detroit. His warriors surrounded and laid siege to the fort. Frustrated British officers discussed giving the Indians blankets infected with the deadly disease smallpox. But the officers rejected the idea, fearing the disease might spread to the British themselves. The fort successfully held out until reinforcements arrived.

Although his siege of Detroit failed, Pontiac inspired other tribes to attack British forts throughout the region. More than two thousand settlers died in this uprising, which the British referred to as Pontiac's Conspiracy. Pontiac later eluded two major British expeditions sent to find and capture him. He remained free until a Peoria Indian shot him in the back in 1769.

The Iroquois and the U.S. Constitution

After the American Revolution, the new American government operated under rules called the Articles of Confederation. But these rules were inadequate to govern the growing country. In considering a better permanent structure for the government, American leaders looked for workable ideas in British and other European law. They also observed the way some Indians structured their ruling councils.

Thomas Jefferson, Benjamin Franklin, and other Americans noted that the Iroquois had a confederacy, or alliance, of five tribes. These tribes, including the Mohawk, Onondaga, Seneca, Oneydoe, and Cayuga, worked together as a republic. This is a nation whose laws are voted on by representatives of the people. Each tribe sent delegates to regular meetings of all the tribes. Iroquois leaders listened to the delegates' suggestions and demands and could do little without the permission of their people.

The Iroquois political system greatly impressed the American founding fathers. Franklin remarked that it would be strange if several different Indian nations could form a working confederacy "and yet that a like union should be impractical for ten or a dozen English colonies...." The Americans went on to combine some Iroquois concepts with those from Europe and their own original ideas. The result was the U.S. Constitution, ratified in 1789 and considered one of the greatest documents in history. The Iroquois received no credit or recognition for their contribution to American government.

Representatives of the Iroquois League meet with the governor of Canada in 1684. Thomas Jefferson adopted some of the tenets of the Iroquois political system when writing the Declaration of Independence.

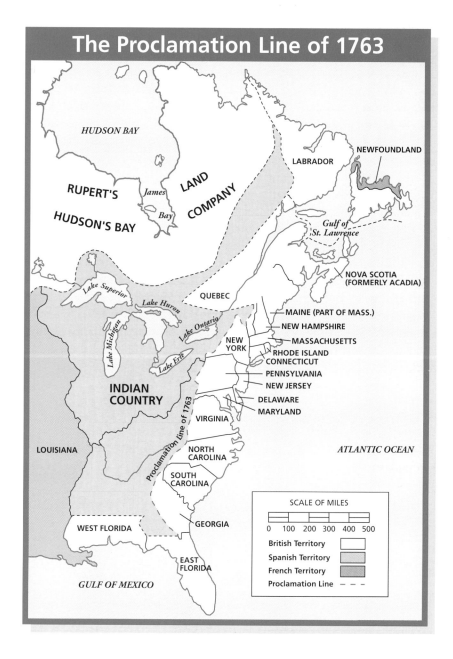

The Proclamation Line of 1763

HUDSON BAY

RUPERT'S
HUDSON'S BAY

LAND
COMPANY

James
Bay

LABRADOR

NEWFOUNDLAND

Gulf of
St. Lawrence

NOVA SCOTIA
(FORMERLY ACADIA)

QUEBEC

Lake Superior

Lake Huron

Lake Michigan

Lake Ontario

Lake Erie

MAINE (PART OF MASS.)

NEW HAMPSHIRE

MASSACHUSETTS

NEW
YORK

RHODE ISLAND
CONNECTICUT

PENNSYLVANIA

NEW JERSEY

INDIAN
COUNTRY

Proclamation Line of 1763

DELAWARE

MARYLAND

VIRGINIA

LOUISIANA

NORTH
CAROLINA

ATLANTIC OCEAN

SOUTH
CAROLINA

WEST FLORIDA

GEORGIA

EAST
FLORIDA

GULF OF MEXICO

SCALE OF MILES

0   100   200   300   400   500

British Territory
Spanish Territory
French Territory
Proclamation Line   – – –

allow the British to spend less money to protect colonists from Indian attack. This would reduce contact and, therefore, confrontations between Indians and whites. The British claimed that all land west of the Appalachians would remain permanent Indian territory. According to the proclamation, whites could obtain Indian land only through special treaties. Most Indians who lived in the Ohio Valley were pleased with this arrangement, believing it would protect their lands and way of life.

The British leaders who drew the Proclamation Line wanted to avoid conflict between Indians and whites and bring peace to the frontier. But many British colonists resented the boundary.

They felt it restricted their freedom to move anywhere they chose. And the population of the colonies was growing rapidly, creating a rising demand for new land. The boundary was one of the grievances that led the colonists to declare their independence and establish the United States only a few years later. Early U.S. leaders did not feel bound by the commitments made by the British. American leaders abolished the Proclamation Line and encouraged white settlement of the Ohio Valley.

A similar scenario would be repeated many times in future relations between Indians and Americans. Like the British in 1763, U.S. government leaders would designate lands beyond a certain boundary as Indian territory. Each American administration would express the hope that its own frontier disputes with the Indians would be the last. But most Americans did not foresee the rapid increases in their own population that would fuel increasing white expansion into Indian lands. This expansion would cause new Indian land disputes. And each new U.S. president would not feel bound to uphold the deals made with the Indians by his predecessors.

CHAPTER TWO

The Old Northwest: Jefferson's World or Tecumseh's?

P rior to the Revolutionary War, thanks to the British Proclamation Line of 1763, there was little white colonial expansion into the territory directly west of the Appalachian
Mountains. So most of the lands of the Ohio Valley and southern Canada were still used primarily by the Indians. Inhabiting
the region were the Ottawa, Chippewa, Shawnee, Potawatomi,
and several dozen other tribes. North American Indians lived
lightly upon the land. Some held small farms and grew corn
and other vegetables. Others hunted and fished and used the
skins and bones of animals for clothes, tools, and weapons.
Often, they moved their villages from season to season in
response to changes in the weather or the movements of herds
of game.

When settlers won their war of independence, however, they
eliminated the British proclamation boundary. This left the Ohio
Valley and Great Lakes region, an area referred to as the Northwest Territory, open for white settlement. The new government
encouraged settlers to move past the Proclamation Line, but it
maintained the line for Indians. Indians could not move back
across the line or travel into white settlements on the former
British-owned side of the line.

Jefferson's World

In the late 1780s, the westward expansion of the infant United
States began in earnest. It was a mass migration that would not
stop until white Americans controlled all the lands from the

Atlantic to the Pacific oceans. Thousands of farmers, trappers, and adventurers began to move across the Appalachians into the Ohio Valley. In 1787, to encourage this expansion, the U.S. government passed the Northwest Ordinance, authored by Thomas Jefferson. This law stated that settlers could move into the Northwest Territory and apply for statehood when their populations grew to sixty thousand. Jefferson and other U.S. leaders assumed that enough settlers would move into the region to create three to five new states.

Jefferson envisioned this westward settlement as necessary for the growth and prosperity of the United States. He saw the future United States as a vast land made up mostly of small farms. These farms would increase the value of the land because they would produce food and other goods to support the general population. The farmers themselves, independent and hardworking, would be model citizens setting an example for the rest of the country. "Those that labor in the earth," Jefferson wrote, "are the chosen people of God, if ever He had a chosen people."

Beginning in the late 1780s, white settlers moved westward in great numbers. Here, frontier settlers prepare to homestead a piece of land.

Jefferson and other leaders knew that there would be disputes with the Indians over frontier lands. But, Jefferson believed that God had created these rich lands to be used and developed by white Christians. He also accepted the belief that the Indians did not own the land because they did not attempt to develop it. Those who were willing and able to develop it, he held, should rightfully lay claim to it. Nevertheless, Jefferson firmly believed that the land should be acquired in a lawful manner. The Northwest Ordinance, for example, provided that Indian land be purchased through official treaties. The ordinance also stated that settlers could not take Indian land "unless in lawful wars authorized by Congress."

As to where the Indians would go after the whites had taken their land, Jefferson looked farther west. He assumed that because the Indians lived off the land, they could live anywhere. He and other American leaders did not recognize that Indian tribes had established tribal boundaries. Each tribe also had traditional enemies who would not appreciate other tribes moving into their territories. Jefferson believed that there was room enough on the continent for both whites and Indians. Each group, he envisioned, would be able to live and prosper within its own designated territory for centuries to come. Said Jefferson, North America had "room enough for our descendants to the hundredth and thousandth generation."

To make room for his nation of farmers, Jefferson set about acquiring vast stretches of western land. In 1803, he was able to purchase from the French the land stretching north to south from Lake Superior to the Gulf of Mexico and east to west from the Mississippi River to the Rocky Mountains. Called the Louisiana Purchase, it covered nearly 830,000 square miles, or more than five million acres, and instantly doubled the size of the United States.

Jefferson told delegations of Indians that they could now move west of the Mississippi River and not be bothered by the whites who fought with them in the eastern states. "We have lately obtained from the French…," said Jefferson, "all the country beyond the Mississippi called Louisiana, in which there is a great deal of land unoccupied by any red men. But it is very far off, and we would prefer giving you lands there…[in exchange] for such parts of your land on this side of the Mississippi as you are disposed to part with." Jefferson did not understand that many tribes already occupied the lands west of the Mississippi. And he still continued to assume that undeveloped lands were not being used. In reality, although their populations were relatively small, the western Indians needed much of the open plains and other lands for hunting. Jefferson also did not take into account that western Indians would resent eastern Indians entering their territories.

Thomas Jefferson wanted to build a nation of small, independent-minded farmers.

Captured by the Indians

When white settlers started moving westward into lands previously occupied by the Indians, they of course were in great danger of being attacked by Indians defending their right to the land. When Indians attacked, either by ambushing a wagon train or by attacking a frontier village, they would often kill all the whites. Sometimes, however, particularly if they needed to replenish their numbers, the Indians would take white captives and adopt them into their tribe. The Indians particularly would adopt young children, women, and sometimes young men. Many whites who managed to escape or who were released after their captivity published narratives of their tenure with the Indians. The accounts and information related here are taken from a collection called *Captured by the Indians* edited by Frederick Drimmer.

In spite of the drawings from the time that appear to attest otherwise, women abducted by the Indians were not usually treated harshly. As

Mary Rowlandson, who was taken captive in Massachusetts by the Wampanoags and Narraganset in King Philip's War in 1676, attests: "I have been in the midst of those roaring lions and savage bears that feared neither God, nor man, nor the devil, by night and day, alone and in company, sleeping all sorts together, and yet not one of them ever offered the least abuse of unchastity to me in word or action." Even Gen. James Clinton, who warred against the Iroquois in New York in 1779, said, "Bad as the savages are, they never violate the chastity of any of their women prisoners."

This may have been because of cultural tenets and not kindness, however. Frederick Drimmer writes, "It was a custom for the braves

Both of these illustrations depict Indian "savages" abducting helpless whites. It was fairly common for Indians to take some whites captive after a battle. During the peak years of white expansion into Indian lands, however, both sides were guilty of improper conduct.

to make elaborate preparations before going on the warpath, and these included the practice of continence and rites of purification. To abuse a female captive would have weakened the Indians' medicine. Moreover, a woman's body was generally held to belong to herself alone, and this principle was extended to white women brought back to live with the tribe."

Some white captives became so attached to their adopted Indian families that they did not want to leave once they were freed by whites who found them. When Col. Henry Bouquet, after Pontiac's War in 1764, signed a peace treaty with Ohio Indians that included giving up their white prisoners, he described the painful parting. He claimed that "The Shawnees were obliged to bind several of their prisoners and force them along to the [white] camp; and some

women, who had been delivered up, found means to escape and run back to the Indians."

Many whites were not safe once abducted, however. The majority of whites who fell into the hands of the Indians were killed. Many captives' accounts relate that during rituals when Indians would tell of the many wrongs done to them by whites, the Indians would torture or sacrifice their white captives. As Charles Johnston, a prisoner of the Shawnee, witnessed, "It is their practice to repeat the injuries inflicted on them by their enemies the whites: to tell how their lands were taken from them—their villages burnt—their cornfields laid waste— their fathers and brothers killed—their women and children carried into captivity." There was certainly cruelty on both sides.

Women and Children

FALLING VICTIMS TO THE

INDIAN'S TOMAHAWK.

The covers of these dime novels feature the true life tales of Indian abductions of whites. Part of the Indians' motivation to take white captives was to replace members of their tribe who had died.

Tecumseh's World

The Indians' opinion of who should control the Northwest Territory and the lands beyond contrasted sharply with that of Jefferson. Indian leaders viewed white encroachment with resentment and concern. The Indians felt that whites would not share the land. Instead, they saw that whenever whites moved into an area, the Indians eventually disappeared from that area. Thus, the Indians increasingly began to recognize that the westward expansion of whites was a direct threat to the Indian way of life. This view was best defined and preached by the Shawnee chief Tecumseh, who was born in about 1768 near the current site of Springfield, Ohio. As Tecumseh grew up, white settlers were pouring into the Ohio Valley. Because of disputes over land, violence between whites and Indians occurred frequently. Tecumseh's father and older brothers were killed by whites who stole Shawnee land.

After dealing with and fighting against whites for many years, Tecumseh became convinced that the westward march of white civilization had to be stopped. He reasoned that white expansion would continue and even increase. Unlike Jefferson, Tecumseh foresaw that there would not be enough frontier land

Tecumseh (astride horse) in a fight with white settlers. Tecumseh was a great leader who inspired confidence and loyalty in his tribe.

Tecumseh's Fight Begins in Childhood

Tecumseh formed his negative view of whites when he was very young. At the age of six, he and his mother found the body of his father, who was killed in Lord Dunsmore's War in 1774. Soon afterward, to escape the fighting on the frontier, Tecumseh's mother and many other Shawnees fled west across the Mississippi River. Tecumseh was raised by his mother and older brother Cheeseekau. Tecumseh had three other brothers, two of whom died fighting whites. The third and youngest brother was Laulewasika. He fell into a trance in 1805 and awoke claiming to be able to foresee the future. He became known as the Prophet.

When Tecumseh was fifteen, he fought in his first battle. At the sight of blood, he turned and ran. Lying in his lodge, ashamed of his cowardice, he vowed he would never again run from an enemy. A few years later, on a buffalo hunt, he fell from his horse and suffered a broken thigh, which would cause him to limp for the rest of his life. So he worried about becoming a successful warrior. Nevertheless, his unusual courage and intelligence enabled him to become a prominent warrior and leader in his tribe by the time he was twenty.

Tecumseh's struggle with white society was not confined to the battlefield. As a young man, he had an association with a white woman that taught him much about the way white people lived. In the 1790s, he met Rebecca Galloway, the young daughter of an Ohio pioneer. He became romantically attached to her, and she taught him to speak English. She also introduced him to the Bible, Shakespeare, and world history. With her father's permission, Tecumseh sought Rebecca's hand in marriage. But she would only agree if he would join white society. After agonizing for over a month, he decided to remain with and fight for the future of his own people.

The Shawnee warrior Tecumseh wanted all Indian tribes to form a united front against white expansion. He foresaw, correctly, that unless the Indians took a stand against whites, they would take over all the land.

to accommodate both Indians and whites. Tecumseh came to believe that no one tribe could stand up to the great numbers of whites. Therefore, the only way that the whites could be stopped and Indian ways of life protected was for all Indians to unite. Tecumseh realized that the task of unifying so many tribes would be difficult. Most tribes had different languages and customs. Many preferred living separately and did not want to unite with other tribes. Nevertheless, Tecumseh dreamed of forging one mighty alliance of all the tribes from Canada to the Gulf of Mexico.

Working to bring about this alliance, Tecumseh traveled frequently across the frontier preaching his ideas to various tribes. He encouraged the Indians to keep their lands and to fiercely resist white treaties and negotiations. He formed an alliance with the British against the Americans, even though the Shawnee had once opposed the British. Tecumseh recognized that the Americans, who had recently broken free of Britain, were now a major threat to the Indians. He also knew that the British wanted to limit American expansion into the Northwest Territory because they wanted to maintain British influence there. He reasoned that siding with the British against the United States would be in the Indians' best interests.

Little Turtle's War

Tecumseh's first major military encounter with U.S. troops occurred in 1790. In an attempt to stop white encroachment by intimidating settlers, the Indians of the Northwest Territory had been periodically raiding white settlements for several years. President George Washington sent soldiers to punish the Indians and restore order to the region. The Miami chief Little Turtle managed to organize several local tribes to oppose these troops. In addition to the Miamis, Little Turtle's forces consisted of Shawnee, Potawatomi, and Chippewa warriors. Tecumseh became a prominent leader of the alliance. The British supplied the Indians with weapons, food, and other supplies. Little Turtle, Tecumseh, and the British all had the same goal—to keep the Americans out of the Ohio Valley. This would preserve the Northwest Territory for the use of the Indians and their British allies.

Late in 1790, about 1,400 U.S. troops led by Gen. Josiah Harmer marched into the Ohio Valley. Tecumseh and Little Turtle pretended to retreat ahead of the soldiers. Thinking that the Indians were afraid, the soldiers became more and more confident. Harmer failed to send out enough scouts to guard against ambushes. Eventually, as the soldiers entered a clearing in the forest, the Indians suddenly attacked from all sides. In less than fifteen minutes, Tecumseh's and Little Turtle's warriors killed 183 soldiers and wounded another 31. There were few Indian casualties, and Harmer quickly retreated.

The Custom of Scalping

Scalping, the removal of part or all of the scalp along with the hair, was commonly practiced by North American Indians in frontier warfare. Many white trappers and frontiersmen also practiced scalping. Although most American Indian tribes took scalps, the custom was most widespread among the eastern and southern Indians. For example, the Creeks and Choctaws, who inhabited the lands bordering the Gulf of Mexico, considered scalping essential. They believed that a young man had to take a scalp in order to become a full-fledged warrior. They also held that the spirits of their ancestors could not rest in peace unless enemy scalps adorned their lodges. Most tribes of the midwestern plains considered scalping less important. They believed that stealing an enemy's horse or touching an enemy's living body were better tests for warriors. These acts were more dangerous and, therefore, took more courage. When they did take scalps, they often used them to decorate their clothing, weapons, or horses.

The practice of scalping became much more widespread among the Indians in the 1700s because of the influence of white European settlers. Whites introduced firearms, which caused more deaths and, therefore, more opportunities for scalping. The whites also introduced metal knives, which made scalping easier and more efficient. In addition, the French, Spanish, British, and Dutch all offered bounties of money or other valuables to Indians for collecting scalps of both Indian and white enemies.

(Left) This woodcut criticizes the British practice of trading firearms and supplies to Indians in exchange for American scalps. The British encouraged Indians to attack colonists both during the Revolutionary War and the War of 1812. (Above) An Indian scalps a white settler.

Washington then sent Gen. Arthur St. Clair, a Revolutionary War hero and governor of the Northwest Territory, to subdue Little Turtle and Tecumseh. Between March and November 1791, St. Clair led 2,000 troops along the Upper Wabash River in western Ohio. Because of insufficient food, morale became so low that some 600 of St. Clair's men deserted before encountering the Indians. Tecumseh's scouts watched the rest of St. Clair's troops advance. At dawn on November 4, 1791, Tecumseh and Little Turtle led another surprise attack on the U.S. soldiers. The three-hour battle ended in the most one-sided Indian victory since the Indian Wars had begun. The U.S. soldiers counted 630 killed and 300 wounded, while Indian casualties numbered less than 100.

Embarrassed by the defeats of Harmer and St. Clair, President Washington sent Gen. Anthony Wayne with more than 3,000 troops to Ohio. In 1794, Wayne established two forts in Indian territory near the site of St. Clair's defeat. During the two months the forts were under construction, Wayne kept them guarded twenty-four hours a day by hundreds of sentries and dozens of cannons. When the forts were completed, Little Turtle tried to lay siege to them but found them too well fortified. He eventually came to the conclusion that, even with British help, he could not stop the American advance, and he advocated making peace. But many of the Indians, including Tecumseh, rejected this idea.

When Little Turtle refused to fight, Tecumseh and two other chiefs, Turkey Foot and Blue Jacket, decided to make a stand against Wayne's troops. The Indians chose to fight in an area known as Fallen Timbers, near the Maumee River on the western shore of Lake Erie. There, a tornado had earlier destroyed a forest, leaving huge twisted tree trunks sprawled across the countryside. The Indians believed that the downed trees would provide ideal cover from which to fight a battle. About 2,000 warriors faced Wayne's army of 3,500. Wayne ordered his men to fire their muskets, then attack with bayonets. The Indians fought back heroically but were overwhelmed by the American charge. This time, the battle was one-sided in favor of the Americans. Hundreds of Indians perished, while the Americans lost only 38 men.

The Battle of Fallen Timbers was an important turning point in the history of frontier warfare. The Indians had failed to keep the Americans out of the Ohio Valley, and white settlers now poured into the area. The whites believed they were within their rights. The Northwest Ordinance had given them the right to take frontier lands either by war or treaty. They had just fought and won a war they believed the Indians had started. From the American point of view, a written treaty would now make the land officially a part of the United States. One year after their defeat, most of the local chiefs, feeling they had no choice, agreed to sign a treaty at Fort Greenville in Ohio. The treaty granted all of Ohio and much of Indiana to the United States. But Tecumseh refused to sign the treaty. It was the whites, he said, and not the Indians who had started all the trouble. He vowed to continue to attempt to unite all Indian tribes and carry on the fight against the advancing Americans.

Tecumseh's Struggle

To promote his Indian alliance, Tecumseh traveled for several years. He went to the lands of the Ottawa and other Canadian tribes. He also visited the Creeks, Choctaws, and Chickasaws in the Mississippi Territory south of Tennessee. "The whites," said Tecumseh, "are already nearly a match for us all united, and too strong for any one tribe alone to resist." Strength, he insisted, could only come through cooperation. "Unless every tribe unanimously combines to give check to the ambition and avarice [greed] of the whites," he said, "they will soon conquer us apart and disunited, and we will be driven away from our native country and scattered as autumnal leaves before the wind."

The alternative to unification, Tecumseh said, would be extermination. "Where today are the Pequod?" he asked. "Where the Narragansets, the Mohawks, Pocanokets, and many other once powerful tribes of our race? They have vanished before the…white men, as snow before a summer sun." Tecumseh warned that the whites would change the land. "Soon their broad roads will pass over the graves of your fathers, and the places of their rest will be blotted out forever. The annihilation of our race is at hand unless we unite in one common cause against the common foe."

In 1808, Tecumseh and the Prophet gathered many warriors together in a village known as Prophet's Town. The village stood near the mouth of Tippecanoe Creek on the Wabash River near the present site of Lafayette, Indiana. William Henry Harrison, then governor of the Indiana Territory, worried as he watched the Shawnee brothers attract many Indian allies to the region. Harrison represented President James Madison, Jefferson's successor. Like Jefferson, Madison wanted to keep the northwest frontier open to settlement by white farmers. Tecumseh's growing alliance, Harrison concluded, might lead to war, posing a threat to this settlement.

Harrison saw that this threat was real when he arranged a treaty with the Miami and Delaware Indians to purchase a large section of Indiana. Although no Shawnee land was involved, the treaty angered Tecumseh. He visited Harrison in 1810 and vowed that he would see to it that the Indians ignored the treaty. He explained that the Indians did not believe in selling

Tecumseh's brother, the Prophet, believed that he and his men had supernatural powers over whites. Because of this belief, the Prophet disobeyed his brother and led his men in battle against whites before reinforcements arrived.

land. "Sell a country!" he shouted. "Why not sell the air, the clouds and the great sea as well as the earth? Did not the Great Spirit make them all for the use of his children?" Tecumseh boldly told Harrison that he planned another trip to the south to bring additional tribes into his alliance.

Knowing that Tecumseh would be away, Harrison decided to attack Prophet's Town and eliminate what he saw as a growing Indian menace. In early November 1811, he led a force of nine hundred American troops to Tippecanoe Creek. Tecumseh had warned the Prophet to avoid a premature battle before the Indian alliance was complete. But the rash and overconfident Prophet decided to attack anyway. On the morning of November 7, he ordered two thousand warriors to assault the American camp. He assured his followers that he had cast a spell over the enemy. Half were already dead, he said, and the other half driven insane. It would be an easy matter to attack and finish them off. Believing the Prophet, the Indians ran headlong at the Americans instead of seeking the cover of rocks and trees as they normally would have. Wave after wave of Indians fell before U.S.

(Above and right) William Henry Harrison, governor of the Indiana Territory, grew suspicious and fearful of Tecumseh and his growing Indian alliance.

In this illustration, the Prophet's tribe runs in a headlong attack upon Harrison's well-equipped soldiers. Believing themselves invincible, the Indians did not take cover behind rocks and trees as they normally would. The ill-advised attack left the Prophet's tribe decimated.

musket fire. The Indians were defeated, the Prophet fled, and Harrison burned Prophet's Town to the ground.

Tecumseh returned in 1812 to find his brother and a few followers living in the ruins of Prophet's Town. Angry that the Prophet had disobeyed orders and hurt the cause of an Indian alliance, Tecumseh disowned his brother. The Indian defeat had disheartened many northern and southern tribes who were looking to Tecumseh for leadership against the whites. The defeat also inspired many Indians in the northwest to seek immediate revenge on the Americans. Many isolated attacks on white settlements followed, with various groups of Indians acting on their own. This was common practice among widely scattered tribes and bands, who lacked unity and rarely followed a single overall commander. Tecumseh disapproved of these raids because they accomplished little and were not part of a coordinated plan.

Tecumseh in the War of 1812

Tecumseh was correct in asserting that the revenge attacks on white settlers worked against the Indians' cause. Settlers began to resent all Indians. Many whites living in the Ohio Valley believed that Tecumseh and the British were purposely directing the attacks. Some sections of this frontier, such as Ohio and Tennessee, had become states in the 1790s and early 1800s. The congressmen who represented these states became fanatically anti-Indian and anti-British. These lawmakers, who championed Jefferson's and Madison's citizen-farmers, were popularly known as the "war hawks." The hawks advocated going to war against Britain and its Indian allies. In fact, the anti-British sentiment stirred up by the hawks became one of the major contributing factors in the U.S. declaration of war against Britain in June 1812.

U.S. soldiers surrender at Fort Detroit.

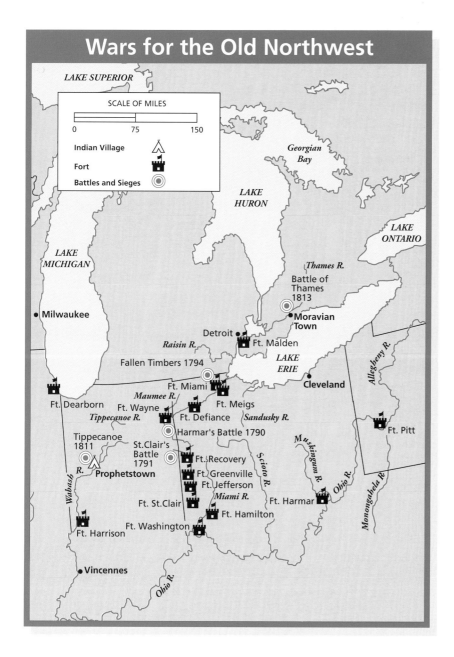

Wars for the Old Northwest

LAKE SUPERIOR

SCALE OF MILES

0 75 150

Indian Village

Fort

Battles and Sieges

Georgian Bay

LAKE HURON

LAKE ONTARIO

LAKE MICHIGAN

Thames R.
Battle of Thames 1813

• Milwaukee

• Moravian Town

Detroit ••
Raisin R.
Ft. Malden

LAKE ERIE

Allegheny R.

Fallen Timbers 1794

Ft. Miami
Maumee R.
Ft. Wayne
Ft. Defiance
Ft. Meigs
Sandusky R.

• Cleveland

Ft. Dearborn
Tippecanoe R.

Harmar's Battle 1790

Ft. Pitt

Tippecanoe 1811
St.Clair's Battle 1791
Ft. Recovery

Muskingum R.

Scioto R.

Prophetstown
Wabash R.
Ft. Greenville
Ft. Jefferson
Miami R.

Ft. Harmar
Ohio R.

Monongahela R.

Ft. St.Clair
Ft. Hamilton

Ft. Harrison
Ft. Washington

• Vincennes

Ohio R.

In this conflict, the United States attempted to expel the British from Canada, while the British tried to keep the United States from expanding farther westward.

Tecumseh was pleased when the war broke out. He saw the conflict between the United States and Britain as an opportunity for the Indians to hold on to the frontier. He believed that the combined military forces of the British and Indians had a chance of defeating the Americans. Tecumseh quickly joined Britain's general Isaac Brock on the shore of Lake Erie, and they planned an assault on Fort Detroit, which U.S. soldiers had recently reinforced. After the soldiers surrendered the fort, Indians helped the

In this somewhat fanciful illustration, Tecumseh and William Henry Harrison challenge each other to a duel.

British capture Fort Mackinac on Lake Michigan. Here, more than half of the British force was made up of Sioux, Winnebagos, Menominees, and Ottawas. These victories gave the British control over Lakes Erie and Michigan. They also inspired many tribes, from the Great Lakes to the Mississippi Territory in the south, to join Tecumseh's alliance.

By 1813, Tecumseh had used these successes to gather together a force of more than three thousand warriors. He helped the British defeat several units of American troops, including small contingents of an army led by William Henry Harrison. By this time, however, the able British leader Isaac Brock had been killed and replaced by the far less talented Henry Proctor. Tecumseh did not get along well with Proctor, who often retreated when Tecumseh thought it was best to attack. Proctor also allowed his soldiers, British and Indians alike, to scalp and murder prisoners. Tecumseh found such behavior disgusting and unethical, and demanded that Proctor explain himself. "Your Indians cannot be controlled," Proctor replied. Said Tecumseh sternly, "I conquer to save and you to murder."

Tecumseh's Last Stand

Tecumseh's frustration with Proctor grew after the American fleet defeated the British fleet on Lake Erie in September 1813. Proctor sensed that the Americans would now attack him at Fort Malden on the western shore of the lake, and he prepared to retreat. Tecumseh wanted to stand and fight the Americans and accused Proctor of cowardice. If the British planned to run away, Tecumseh said, they should give their guns and ammunition to the Indians to defend their homeland. Proctor finally convinced Tecumseh that a retreat was necessary, promising that the Indians would get their chance to fight the U.S. soldiers later.

On October 5, the U.S. forces under Harrison caught up with Proctor and Tecumseh along the Thames River north of Lake Erie. Proctor wanted to continue running, but Tecumseh insisted it was time to fight. After a devastating charge by mounted U.S. soldiers, many of the British troops, including Proctor, fled. But Tecumseh's Indian forces held their ground, even after being surrounded. After several minutes of fierce hand-to-hand combat,

Well-equipped U.S. cavalry charge the Indian allies of the British. After this devastating charge, many British fled while the Indians continued to fight.

Tecumseh fell, and this so disheartened the Indians that they retreated. After the battle, some U.S. soldiers skinned the body of an Indian they mistakenly believed to be Tecumseh. They wanted to make tobacco pouches and other souvenirs from his skin. That night, several Shawnee warriors crept across the battlefield and recovered the body of the real Tecumseh. They buried him deep in the forest where he could never be found.

Tecumseh's dream of a mighty Indian alliance against the whites died with him. But he left behind an example of courage, discipline, and honor that some Indians later tried to follow. Both Indians and whites recognized Tecumseh as a great leader. Even his enemy Harrison praised him, calling him "one of those uncommon geniuses which spring up occasionally to produce revolutions and overturn the established order of things." Said Harrison, "If it were not for the vicinity of the United States, he would perhaps be the founder of an empire that would rival in glory Mexico [the Aztecs] or Peru [the Incas]."

Tecumseh represented perhaps the last best hope for the Indians to stop the advance of white civilization. After his passing, the Indian tribes of the northwest proved to be too diverse and disunited to stand up against the white advance. Some tribes made peace with the Americans and helped them fight other tribes. The tribes that continued to resist white expansion were defeated one by one. It was now inevitable that Jefferson's prediction about the whites pushing the Indians beyond the Mississippi would come to pass. The Northwest Territory and all the lands east of the Mississippi would follow Jefferson's vision, not Tecumseh's.

CHAPTER THREE

Andrew Jackson
and
Indian Removal

After Tecumseh's death and the end of the War of 1812, no united military resistance remained to stop white settlers from moving west. Most of the northwestern frontier, including Ohio and Indiana, had already been secured from the Indians either by war or treaty. White settlers now looked to the southern frontier, most of which was still inhabited by Indians. This region encompassed the Mississippi Territory, including what is now Alabama, as well as Florida, western Georgia, and parts of Tennessee and Louisiana.

The U.S. government advocated white expansion into these southern lands. Its official viewpoint was that the Indians stood in the way of this expansion, so they would have to be removed, by force if necessary. The tribes would then be relocated to the territories west of the Mississippi, which had come to be called Indian Country. This policy grew out of Jefferson's earlier idea of moving the Indians out of the east and across the Mississippi. The difference was that Jefferson had advocated doing this through treaties while maintaining good relations with the Indians. After decades of bitter and bloody fighting, however, white leaders now felt justified in using harsher means to implement this plan.

The leading U.S. figure to implement the goal of removal of the southern Indian tribes was Andrew Jackson. As a military general during and after the War of 1812, he opposed and defeated many of the tribes in Georgia and Florida. Later, as territorial governor and president, Jackson created and carried out the Indian removal policies of the U.S. government.

Jackson's goal was to create separate living spheres for whites and Indians. Jackson and other white leaders of his day were partly motivated by a belief that Indians were inferior and barbaric. Reportedly, Jackson told some congressional leaders that he agreed with the description of Indians in the Declaration of Independence. The document describes the "merciless Indian savages, whose known rule of warfare is an undistinguished destruction of all ages, sexes, and conditions." Jackson also held that two so completely different cultures could never live together. Most importantly, the Indians stood in the way of white expansion. As historian Irwin Unger put it, Jackson saw Indians as "a nuisance and an impediment to western growth and economic progress."

Like Jefferson, Jackson refused to see that by pushing Indians off their land, he was depriving them of their livelihood. He, too, thought Indians could simply move. Said Jackson, "I suggest…setting apart an ample district west of the Mississippi…to be guaranteed to the Indian tribes, as long as they shall [desire to] occupy it." Regarding the use of force to remove the tribes, he found such actions regrettable but necessary. In the long run, he firmly believed, the policy would be in the best interests of both peoples. But to the Indians, Indian removal caused untold misery and the destruction of entire ways of life. Thousands of people were forced to abandon their homes and move to distant, unfamiliar territories. Today, Indians, as well as many whites, see Indian removal in the 1820s and 1830s as one of the most shameful periods in U.S. history.

Gen. Andrew Jackson oversaw the removal of southern Indian tribes to Indian Country. He advocated separate living spheres for whites and Indians.

The Creek War

The first southern Indians Jackson led U.S. troops against were the Creeks. Most Creeks, who lived in towns scattered throughout Georgia and Alabama in the early 1800s, had remained neutral during the War of 1812. These Lower Creeks, or White Sticks, made peace with the United States. Chief Red Eagle, however, leader of the Upper Creeks, or Red Sticks, believed in Tecumseh's philosophy of Indian resistance against white expansion. Red Eagle, interestingly, was not a full-blooded Indian. Born William Weatherford, he was mostly of Scottish descent. He lived with the Creeks for many years and rose to the rank of chief even though he was only one-eighth Indian. When Tecumseh had visited the Creeks in 1811 and 1812, Red Eagle had joined his Indian-British alliance against the Americans.

In 1813, Red Eagle's warriors began attacking settlers in Alabama. The goal was to strike terror into the hearts of the whites and force them to leave the area. About five hundred frightened settlers took refuge at Fort Mims on the Alabama River about forty-five miles north of the town of Mobile. At noon on August 20, Red Eagle led a war party of one thousand warriors against the small stockade. First, the Creeks fired flaming arrows into the fort. Then the warriors noticed that someone had carelessly left the gate open, and they rushed inside. In the massacre that followed, about four hundred whites died and thirty-six escaped. The Indians spared a few dozen black slaves who were in the fort.

A typical Creek lodge made out of logs. The Creeks were the first southern Indians Jackson attempted to remove to Indian Country.

Indian Territory

efore the whites arrived in North America, most Indians lived within their own lands without clearly defined boundaries. White settlers imposed boundaries on the land and defined private property, an alien concept to the Indians. The Indians did not understand how a person could own things like earth and water, which seemed to exist for the use of all people. The Indians were also confused when the whites kept changing the boundaries.

As white settlements increased in the eastern and southern United States, the Indians were forced onto small pieces of land called reservations. These were usually located in remote and/or desolate areas that whites themselves found unproductive or unappealing. But the white population continued to grow rapidly, and demand for land, often any land, increased.

Frequently, after a tribe adjusted to the boundaries of a reservation, the white authorities decided to make the reservation smaller in order to free more land for whites. Thus, the boundaries the whites forced on the Indians kept changing.

Eventually, Americans laid claim to most eastern land, and there was public demand for the government to stop establishing new reservations in the east. In 1834, the U.S. Congress designated a large part of the west beyond the Mississippi River as Indian Country. This was intended to be territory where Indians could live without interference from whites. At first, Indian Country included large sections of what are now Oklahoma, Kansas, and Nebraska. As the United States expanded, however, American authorities reduced the size of Indian Country

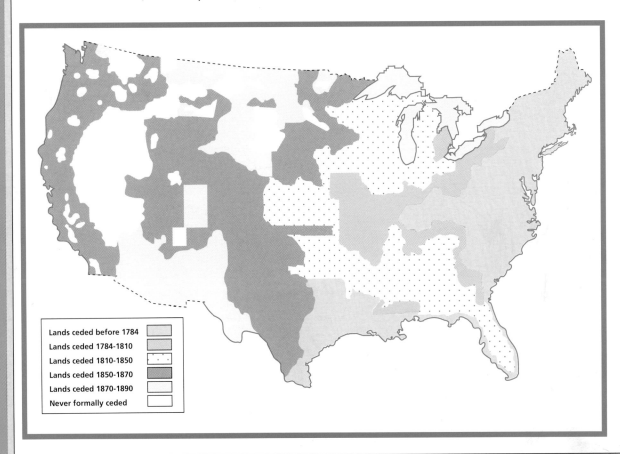

Lands ceded before 1784
Lands ceded 1784-1810
Lands ceded 1810-1850
Lands ceded 1850-1870
Lands ceded 1870-1890
Never formally ceded

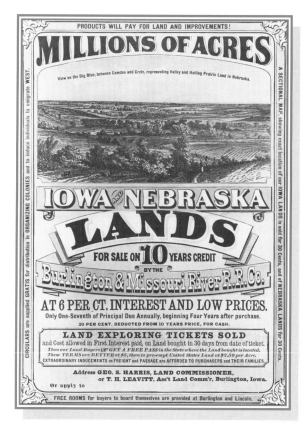

until it consisted only of Oklahoma. Later, Indian lands became smaller still. The Indians who inhabited Indian Country never had any say in where they lived. Instead, whites divided up the land into domains for separate Indian tribes and nations.

Whites moved westward in great numbers during the nineteenth century. (Top) A family poses with the wagon in which they live and travel during their pursuit of a homestead. (Above) Homesteaders wait in line at a land office in hopes of filing a land claim. At left, a poster entices settlers to homestead land in Iowa and Nebraska at bargain prices.

Creeks overrun Fort Mims and massacre the whites who took refuge there. Of the more than five hundred soldiers and settlers in the fort, only a handful escaped.

After receiving word of the massacre, angry Tennessee and Georgia legislators met to decide on how to retaliate. They authorized Gen. Andrew Jackson to lead an army of thirty-five hundred militia against the Red Stick Creeks. The whites were not the only ones angered and repulsed by the Fort Mims attack. Some southern Indians who had before remained neutral felt that Red Eagle had gone too far and should be taught a lesson. More than five hundred Cherokees signed up with Jackson's militia. Some White Stick Creeks, Chickasaws, and Choctaws also aided Jackson.

During the fall of 1813 and winter of 1813-1814, Jackson's forces defeated the Red Stick Creeks in one battle after another. After losing hundreds of warriors, Red Eagle took his remaining force of about 1,200 and searched for a place to make a major stand against Jackson. The Creeks fortified Horseshoe Bend, a small peninsula jutting out into the Tallapoosa River in Alabama. On March 17, 1814, Jackson led a force of 3,000, including some 200 Cherokees, against the Creek stronghold. Among Jackson's men were famed frontiersmen Sam Houston and Davy Crockett. First, the Cherokees swam the river and captured dozens of canoes that the Creeks had placed near shore in case escape became necessary. At noon, Jackson ordered a cannon bombardment, after which his forces attacked. The battle lasted all day and ended with the death of nearly all the Creek warriors. About 300 Creek women and children survived. Fewer than 50 of Jackson's troops were killed and about 150 were wounded.

Red Eagle was not among the Creek dead. By coincidence, he had left the stronghold the day before to inspect other camps. Several days after the battle at Horseshoe Bend, Red Eagle walked into Jackson's camp and asked to see Jackson himself. Approaching the American general, Red Eagle fearlessly announced, "I am Bill Weatherford. I am a soldier. I have done the white people all the harm I could; I have fought them, and fought them bravely; if I had an army, I would yet fight, and contend [resist] to the last; but I have none; my people are all gone. I can now do no more than weep over the misfortunes of my nation." Jackson, out of respect and sympathy, released Weatherford, who walked away never to fight again.

A few months later, on August 9, 1814, Jackson concluded a treaty with the Creeks. Since most of the Red Sticks had been killed or had fled, the Creeks who signed the document were White Sticks, who had supported the United States during the conflict. Jackson held that because of the actions of the Red Sticks, the United States had the right to take nearly all Creek lands. The treaty ceded, or gave, over twenty-three million acres, both Upper and Lower Creek lands in Georgia and Alabama, to the United States. The White Sticks were forced onto small reservations in Alabama.

Davy Crockett (left) and Sam Houston were among the men who joined Andrew Jackson in the fight against the Creeks.

The Seminole Wars

This illustration depicts the typical garb of a Seminole chief.

In the ten years following the 1814 treaty with the Creeks, Andrew Jackson concluded or influenced nine more treaties with southern Indians. Because of these deals, the United States acquired three-fourths of Alabama and Florida, one-third of Tennessee, one-fifth each of Georgia and Mississippi, and some of Kentucky and North Carolina. Most of the Indians who agreed to these deals did so because they felt there was no other choice. They remembered what had happened to the Creeks and realized that it would be futile to fight against the much more powerful United States.

One tribe, however, put up a stiff fight for many years against U.S. expansion. This was the Seminole tribe inhabiting much of northern Florida, which was then a Spanish territory. The U.S. government wanted Florida, but the Spanish did not want to sell it. Although the initial troubles between Americans and Seminoles had nothing to do with the Spanish, U.S. desire for Spanish land became the main U.S. goal of the war. Fighting the Seminoles provided the United States with an excuse to send military forces into Florida to intimidate the Spanish.

No more than five thousand Seminoles lived in Florida. But they put up such fierce resistance that they occupied the U.S. Army for seven years and were never entirely defeated or officially removed from the region. Tensions first arose between the Seminoles and the United States in a series of minor incidents. In 1814, the Seminoles encouraged their Red Stick Creek neighbors to fight the Americans. After the Creek War ended, the Seminoles gave shelter to some Red Sticks who had escaped to Florida. Finally, in 1816, some Seminole warriors were accused of murdering whites in southern Georgia. It remains unclear whether the charge was true, but the chief of the village where the warriors lived refused to give them up to white authorities. In response, U.S. general Edmund P. Gaines led several hundred troops across the border into Spanish territory. The Americans forced the Indians out of the village, then destroyed it along with all of its supplies.

The destruction of the Seminole village enraged all Seminoles, angered local Spanish authorities, and increased violent incidents in northern Florida. In one incident, the Indians attacked a boat containing U.S. soldiers' families on the Apalachicola River in southern Georgia. Several women and children were killed. This convinced the U.S. War Department that the Seminoles were a significant threat to white settlements in the region. The department sent Andrew Jackson, whose reputation as war hero and Indian fighter was now renowned, to take charge of U.S. forces in Georgia.

There was another reason for sending Jackson to Florida. For years, Jackson had publicly advocated acquiring Florida from the Spanish, by force if necessary. Although U.S. officials did not directly order him to capture Florida, they expected the impetuous Jackson to do just that. Shortly after arriving in Georgia, he accused the Spanish of encouraging the Seminoles to attack American settlers. This charge was untrue but gave Jackson an excuse for moving against the Spanish while he dealt with the Indians. In 1817, and again in 1818, he boldly crossed the border and attacked Indian and Spanish towns in northern Florida. During these attacks, Jackson failed to capture many Indians or significantly weaken Seminole resistance. But he was very successful against the Spanish, who had few forts or troops in Florida. Jackson assaulted and captured the Spanish fort at Pensacola. He justified this action on the grounds that the Spanish had failed to control the Indians in their own territory. The Spanish did not wish to become involved in a war with the United States. To avoid further trouble, they sold Florida to the United States for $5 million in 1819. In 1821, Jackson became governor of the newly created Florida Territory.

Seminoles attack an American fort in 1837. Although few in number, the Seminoles put up a fierce resistance to whites' efforts to remove them from their land.

Jackson, sanctioned by the U.S. government, now insisted that the Seminoles leave Florida and relocate to lands west of the Mississippi. Despite repeated threats by U.S. officials and the influx of thousands of American settlers into Florida, the Seminoles refused to move. When Jackson became president of the United States in 1829, he stepped up his pressure on the Seminoles. Over the next few years, there were a number of battles and incidents between Americans and Seminoles. The most celebrated incident occurred in 1837, when U.S. officials tricked Seminole chief Osceola with an invitation to a phony peace council. Soldiers captured Osceola and locked him in a South Carolina prison, where he died of malaria a year later.

Between 1835 and 1842, the U.S. government shipped about three thousand Seminoles to Indian Country beyond the Mississippi. But more than two thousand Seminoles remained. Most moved deep into the Florida swamps where the whites could find them only with great difficulty. Some of the descendants of these Seminoles continue to occupy remote areas of Florida.

Indian Removal Begins

Although the removal of the Seminoles was only partly successful, removal of some other tribes proceeded with much greater efficiency. Some of the major tribes affected were the Cherokees, Choctaws, Chickasaws, and Creeks. Along with the Seminoles, these became known as the "five civilized tribes." They earned this nickname because, until the early 1800s, they had gotten along well with white Europeans and easily adopted many white ways. For instance, they had carried on a thriving trade with the Spanish, French, and British on the Atlantic coast. And they had also learned to plant grains and garden vegetables and to raise horses, cattle, hogs, and chickens.

Many whites looked upon the Cherokees as the most civilized of all the Indians in the region. The Cherokees provided a textbook picture of Jefferson's ideal nation of hardworking, peaceful farmers. In the early 1800s, the Cherokees adopted many white institutions. Each tribe wrote a constitution, passed laws, and established churches. Some even acquired plantations complete with slaves. Most became literate, thanks to a written alphabet invented by a Cherokee named Sequoyah.

Despite the efforts of the Cherokees, Choctaws, and other tribes to learn white ways, Jackson and other U.S. officials began to pressure them to relocate beyond the Mississippi. To Jackson, although these Indians seemed more civilized than others, they were still Indians. He, along with most other American leaders, felt that all Indians stood in the way of white civilization. Jackson made it plain that sooner or later the Cherokees and others would have to move. In 1817, to avoid fighting,

The Death of Osceola

A young Seminole leader named Osceola achieved national prominence in 1835 for his dramatic opposition to relocation to Indian Country. At first, Osceola thought it best to avoid war and signed a treaty agreeing to leave Florida. But soon afterward he changed his mind, deciding that war would be more honorable than abandoning his native homeland. Osceola challenged the whites in a conflict that became known as the Second Seminole War.

In all of the battles fought between Osceola and U.S. forces, the whites lost more men than the Indians. In December 1835, Osceola ambushed and killed an American general and four other soldiers in northern Florida. On New Year's Eve, Osceola and another Seminole leader named Alligator surprised eight hundred soldiers on the Withlacoochee River and drove them out of Florida.

Unable to defeat Osceola, the Americans decided to use trickery to capture him. They sent a message to Osceola inviting him to a peace conference. But when the Indians showed up to negotiate, the soldiers captured Osceola and some of his followers. U.S. authorities then sent him to a Florida prison. Later, they transferred him to a South Carolina prison, where he contracted malaria.

Osceola's bravery and military prowess inspired not only other Indians, but also many whites. As a result, while in captivity, he received much attention and even some sympathy

This portrait of Seminole leader Osceola was painted by Western artist George Catlin in 1837. Unable to defeat the chief and his warriors, U.S. soldiers captured him through trickery.

from the American press. "Treacherous he may have been," wrote a southern newspaper, "but we cannot forget that he was provoked by treachery.... We now owe him the respect which the brave ever feel toward the brave."

some six thousand Cherokees moved voluntarily. They exchanged their South Carolina land for land in the Arkansas Territory, which was a part of Indian Country. Andrew Jackson was appointed military commander of the territory.

The southern Indians encountered many problems in Arkansas, including Indians already inhabiting the region. The local tribes, most notably the Osages, saw the Cherokees as intruders. The two tribes went to war in 1821, and both sides suffered heavy losses. The Choctaws faced similar problems. In 1820, they traded land in Mississippi for land in Arkansas. Like the Cherokees, the Choctaws found themselves at war with the Indians who already laid claim to the lands of Indian Country. Tensions between these eastern and western tribes forced to live together remained for decades.

The pace of Indian removal increased when Jackson became president in 1829. In his first official message to Congress, he emphasized the ongoing Indian problems in the south. He admitted that the Cherokees and several other tribes had made "progress in the arts of civilized life." But the problem, as Jackson saw it, was that the Indians occupied land that the whites needed. Because the two races were so different, he insisted, it was impossible for them to share the land. So the Indians would have to move. Once more, he promised that there was enough land west of the Mississippi for all Indians to live on without interference for "as long as grass grows or water runs in peace and plenty. It will be theirs forever."

Use of Force

Confident that they had the backing of the president, Georgia legislators decided to persuade the tribes to leave faster by imposing harsh restrictions on Indians. The Georgians passed laws stripping Indians of all civil rights. For example, anyone with Indian blood was forbidden to testify in court against a white person. Contracts between Indians and whites were pronounced void unless witnessed by at least two whites. Indians were not allowed to hold public meetings or to dig for gold on their own lands.

Tribes such as the Cherokees were outraged at this blatant discrimination. But they realized that going to war against the whites was useless. So some Cherokees decided to take their grievances to court. They hired two prominent Washington lawyers who took two Cherokee cases to the U.S. Supreme Court. They lost the first case, but in the second, Chief Justice John Marshall declared the repressive Georgia laws unconstitutional. Indian nations, he said, were "domestic dependent nations" that could have independent political communities

Sequoyah and His Alphabet

A young Cherokee genius named Sequoyah saw that his people were at a disadvantage because they did not have a written language. It seemed obvious to him that one of the greatest strengths of white civilization was its written languages. The whites used the printed word for communicating ideas, maintaining records and trade, and spreading new information. These and other functions of writing helped make white civilization efficient and powerful. So Sequoyah decided to invent a written language for the Cherokees.

Beginning in the late 1780s, Sequoyah worked on his language project for more than twelve years. He began with simple Indian pictographs, or drawings, using one graph for each word in the language. After much experimentation, he decided that this approach would not work because it required learning thousands of separate symbols. Then he hit upon the idea of creating a symbol for each distinct sound or syllable in the Cherokee language. He ended up with eighty-five separate symbols, many borrowed from the English, Greek, and Hebrew alphabets.

Sequoyah's written language provoked various reactions. Some of his fellow Cherokees were suspicious of his efforts to copy the "talking leaves" of the whites. A worried Indian even burned Sequoyah's records. But Sequoyah convinced Cherokee leaders that writing was important by showing how his six-year-old daughter had mastered it using his system. White observers were astonished at how quickly young Cherokees learned the new language. After only a few days of study, Cherokee children could read as well as white students who had studied English for one or two years. In only a few months, Sequoyah's entire tribe became literate.

Sequoyah's efforts did not end there. With his help, the Cherokees were able to establish the first Indian newspaper, the *Cherokee Phoenix,* in 1828 in New Echota, Georgia. The paper was printed in both English and Cherokee. As the Cherokees relocated to the lands west of the Mississippi, Sequoyah's language helped eastern and western Cherokees stay in communication. He planned to expand the language to unite the spoken tongues of all American Indians. While traveling to study these cultures, he disappeared without a trace in 1843. His notebooks containing his research on Indian languages were never found.

Sequoyah (below) borrowed the idea of writing from white settlers and, although he could not read, invented his own written language. It used syllable sound signs (bottom) that corresponded to the spoken language of the Cherokee.

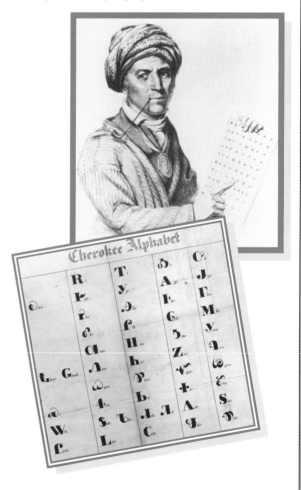

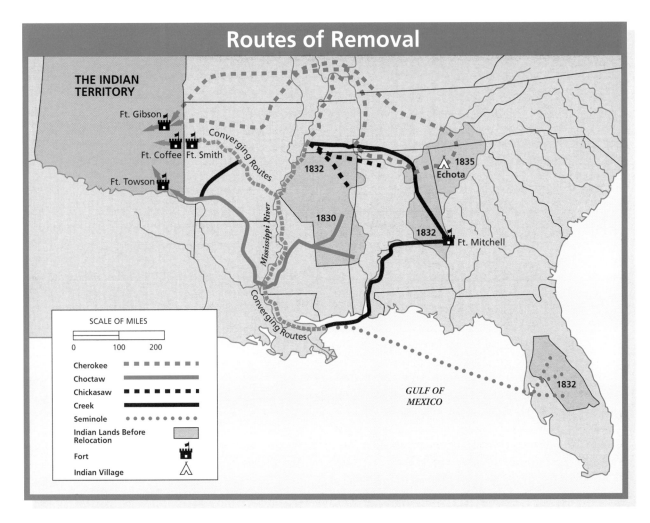

Routes of Removal

THE INDIAN TERRITORY

Ft. Gibson

Ft. Coffee Ft. Smith

Converging Routes

Ft. Towson

Mississippi River

1832

1830

1835 Echota

1832

Ft. Mitchell

Converging Routes

GULF OF MEXICO

1832

SCALE OF MILES

0   100   200

Cherokee

Choctaw

Chickasaw

Creek

Seminole

Indian Lands Before Relocation

Fort

Indian Village

without state restrictions. And they could count on the federal government for protection from unfair actions by the states.

But, despite the high court's decision, the Jackson administration did not enforce the ruling. The president had already made up his mind about Indian removal, and he now told Georgia leaders to ignore the ruling. "John Marshall has made his decision," Jackson reportedly said. "Now let him [try to] enforce it." Jackson was confident because he, not the court, controlled the army, and only the army could force Georgians to obey Marshall's ruling.

After Jackson defied the Supreme Court, Congress felt confident in speeding up Indian removal. It passed the Indian Removal Act in 1830. This act officially began the process of Indian land exchanges with the aim of eventually relocating all Indians west of the Mississippi. In 1834, Congress established specific boundaries for Indian Country. This land covered much of what is now Oklahoma, Nebraska, and Kansas. Said Congress, it would be a permanent Indian reservation in which all Indians could live together forever. The act was significant because the territory it defined as Indian Country was much smaller than the "all lands west of the Mississippi" that American leaders had earlier promised. It was already becoming plain to Americans that U.S. expansion would not stop at the Mississippi River.

Although the removal law said nothing about the use of force, American governors and army officers often resorted to force in order to get Indians to move. When the Creeks in Alabama refused to move, some were dragged away in chains. White soldiers herded many Choctaws out of Mississippi in the dead of winter even though most of the Indians did not have proper winter clothing. Several groups of Cherokees, Creeks, and other southern Indians went through forced removals during the 1830s. On these westward marches, thousands died of sickness and starvation.

The Trail of Tears

Perhaps the largest, most famous Indian removal was that of the Cherokees. Although some had already moved to Indian Country before 1820, many Cherokees continued to resist leaving the lands of their ancestors. They repeatedly tried fighting in the courts, but these attempts failed. The Cherokees also tried the power of the press. In Georgia, the *Cherokee Phoenix,* the first American Indian

(Below, bottom) These paintings depict the suffering of the Cherokee on the "trail of tears," the cruel forced relocation of the Cherokee people.

newspaper, printed articles against white repression and Indian removal. White Georgians promptly stole the paper's printing press and jailed the staff. The Cherokees even tried sending a representative to plead personally with President Jackson. But the president only insisted that Indians could never live among civilized whites. The Cherokees' only remedy, he said, was to move west.

When the Cherokees in Georgia still refused to leave, Jackson's successor, Martin Van Buren, decided to take drastic action. On May 26, 1838, he ordered seven thousand U.S. troops and Georgia state militia under Gen. Winfield Scott to remove the Cherokees by whatever means necessary. Soldiers quietly surrounded Cherokee homes, then surprised and dragged away the occupants. According to historian James Mooney, "Families at dinner were startled by the sudden gleam of bayonets in the doorway and rose to be driven...along the weary miles of trail that led to the stockade [temporary holding place]. Men were seized in their fields or going along the road...and children [taken] from their play." Often, crowds of whites following the soldiers looted and burned the Indians' homes.

Cherokee men, women, and children trudge forward with their belongings and animals on the trail of tears.

A few of the white soldiers were sympathetic to the plight of the Cherokees. Some allowed a family to feed their chickens one last time. Members of another family were permitted to pray quietly in their own language before leaving their home. "I fought in the Civil War and have seen men shot to pieces and slaughtered by the thousands," said one Georgia militiaman many years later. "But the Cherokee removal was the cruelest work I ever knew."

Within one week, the troops rounded up more than seventeen thousand Cherokees and began transporting them west. The survivors of this forced march later called it "the trail of tears." Dozens of Indians died of disease, starvation, or exposure on each day of the long journey. Many had to be buried along the road. More than four thousand Cherokees died before the tribe reached its destination in Indian Country in March 1839.

In all, about sixty thousand members of the five civilized tribes left their homelands never to return. Of these, at least fifteen thousand, mostly women and children, died along the way to Indian Country. By 1840, some Georgians boasted that no Indians remained on their soil, except in the jails. Andrew Jackson, who had been the guiding force behind the removals, remarked that he had settled the Indian problem to everyone's satisfaction. He claimed to have saved the red race from extinction by placing the Indians "beyond the reach of injury or oppression." The government, he said, would "hereafter watch over them and protect them." Though Jackson sincerely believed what he was saying, his words did nothing later to protect the Indians of the Southwest. They were the next group of native Americans to face the relentless tide of white expansion.

President Van Buren ordered the forced removal of the Cherokee people.

CHAPTER FOUR

Wars to Control the Southwest

Between 1846 and 1848, the United States fought and won a war against Mexico. In the treaty that concluded the war, the United States acquired much former Mexican territory, including what are now the states of Arizona and New Mexico, for future settlement. This region became the New Mexico Territory and was also referred to as the American Southwest. At the time, it was inhabited by a few thousand American and Mexican settlers who called themselves New Mexicans. The area was also inhabited by thousands of Indians. The largest tribe in the area was the Navajo, whose members lived in eastern Arizona and western New Mexico.

Differing Views of Southwestern Lands

The Navajos looked upon the Southwest as their homeland, settled by their ancestors at least nine hundred years before. In 1848, there were about twelve thousand Navajos living as independent farmers, shepherds, and hunters. They inhabited homes made of logs and brush. They raised sheep, of which they had as many as 200,000, and horses, which numbered over sixty thousand. The Navajos also grew corn and fruit trees and excelled in the production of buckskin clothing, woven blankets, and other crafts.

The Navajos were also effective fighters. For more than 250 years, they had waged war against the Spanish and later the Mexicans. Because the Spanish and Mexicans claimed and established settlements in Navajo lands, the Indians looked upon them as invaders. The New Mexican settlers, who constantly built ranches and farms on Indian land, also were viewed as invaders by the Navajos. Whites frequently stole Indian sheep and horses. Often, Navajos raided New Mexican farms and settlements to recover lost livestock or for revenge. It was common practice for both Indians and whites to kidnap and hold each other as hostages. The Navajos had Indian enemies, too. These included other southwestern tribes like the Utes, Comanches, Kiowas, and the Apaches. They periodically raided each other's lands.

When the Americans took possession of New Mexico, the Navajos expected them to be new and very welcome allies. After all, both the Americans and Navajos shared the same enemies. Not only had they both opposed the Mexicans, they both hated the Apaches, who raided American settlers as well as Navajo villages. Thus, the Navajos were confused when the Americans, like the New Mexicans before them, began settling on Navajo lands.

The Americans who settled in Navajo territory did so believing that the Indians had no claim to the land. From the American viewpoint, the United States had rightfully acquired the Southwest through its war with Mexico. Many Americans believed that

(Right, bottom) The Navajo lived in the American Southwest hundreds of years before whites. Farmers, shepherds, and hunters, many Navajo were also skilled at crafts such as silversmithing.

Manifest Destiny

Between 1845 and 1848, the United States enlarged its territory by more than one million square miles. Texas became part of the United States in 1845, adding 385,000 square miles. British and American negotiators settled on boundaries for the Oregon Territory in 1846. This area encompassed what are now the states of Oregon, Washington, and Idaho, and added another 283,000 square miles to the United States. In the peace treaty of Guadalupe Hidalgo that ended the Mexican war, the Mexicans had to give up some 531,000 square miles of territory. Included were California, New Mexico, Arizona, Nevada, and parts of Utah and Colorado.

This relentless westward expansion of the United States was coined Manifest Destiny by John O'Sullivan, editor of the popular *Democratic Review* in 1845. According to the Manifest Destiny theory, God intended that white Americans should rule the continent from one ocean to the other. Said O'Sullivan, it is "our manifest destiny to over-spread the continent allotted by Providence [God's will] for the free development of our expanding millions."

Manifest destiny ignored Indians' claim to the land they already inhabited. U.S. authorities did not take Indian land claims very seriously.

such U.S. expansion was inevitable, calling it the country's Manifest Destiny. This was the then-popular idea that it was the United States' God-given fate to eventually stretch from the Atlantic to the Pacific oceans. The official U.S. position was that the United States owned the Southwest, and the rights and desires of American farmers and settlers came first. The Indians of the region would be tolerated so long as they did not cause trouble or get in the way of white settlement.

Troubles with the Navajos Begin

The first American commander of the New Mexico Territory was Stephen W. Kearny. He defined the American attitude toward the southwestern Indians in one of his first public speeches to a gathering of white settlers and merchants. "The Apaches and Navajos come down from the mountains and carry off your sheep and your women whenever they please," Kearny told the New Mexicans. "My government will correct all this. They will keep off the Indians, protect you in your persons and property." Thus, Kearny established the idea that the settlers were the rightful owners of the land, and the Indians, trespassers.

In an attempt to make sure that the Indians stopped harassing the settlers, Kearny invited all the New Mexico tribes to send delegations to him. He demanded that the Indians sign treaties promising that they would maintain the peace. The Utes and

The Navajo inhabited the semi-desert areas of what is now New Mexico. This illustration of a valley inhabited by the Navajo gives a good idea of the type of terrain on which they lived.

many other tribes sent delegations to U.S. Army headquarters in Santa Fe, but the Navajos never came.

Eventually, some U.S. officials journeyed to the New Mexican town of Ojo del Oso to meet with Navajo leaders and get them to sign a treaty. The Navajos said that they were puzzled by the American attitude toward their tribe. Zarcillas Largas, a highly respected Navajo leader, expressed the view that the Americans should help the Navajos fight their mutual enemies. Among these, he said, were the New Mexican settlers who earlier had been Mexican citizens. "You are powerful," Largas told the officials. "You have great guns and many brave soldiers. You have therefore conquered them [the Mexicans], the very thing we have been attempting to do for so many years." The U.S. officials explained that, since the war was over, the Mexicans were no longer enemies. And the Navajos must no longer attack New Mexicans, who were now American citizens.

After much negotiation, the American officials persuaded the Navajos to sign a peace treaty with the United States. "If New Mexico be really in your possession, and it be the intention of your government to hold it, we will cease our depredations [attacks], and refrain from future wars," said Largas. "Let there be peace among us."

Despite the treaty, some Navajos continued stealing livestock from New Mexico settlers. The various Navajo bands had no overall central authority, and many warriors did not feel bound by what Largas and other chiefs had promised the whites. The army assumed that all the Navajos had broken the treaty and decided to teach them a lesson. Army authorities sent several small expeditions against the Navajos, but all of these ended in failure. The Indians knew the land well, especially the areas containing steep canyons. The white soldiers got lost easily and had trouble finding the enemy. Even when the soldiers sighted a band of Navajos, the Indians seemed to disappear into the landscape before the soldiers could attack.

Attempts at Negotiation

In July 1849, American authorities tried a different approach. They sent a negotiator named James S. Calhoun, along with 175 soldiers, to talk with Navajo leaders. While the Americans rested near some Navajo cornfields, several hundred Navajos arrived to meet them. Leading the Indians were three chiefs—Jose Largo, Archuleta, and Narbona. Calhoun scolded the chiefs for ignoring the first treaty and demanded that they give up thievery and return all stolen property. The Indian leaders replied that they could not control all the thieves among their people. But they would try. Most Navajos, they insisted, wanted peace, and they agreed to sign a new treaty.

Indian Fighters

There was a major difference in the fighting styles of the Navajos and white soldiers. Indian fighters were free to follow their own instincts and exercise their own judgment in dangerous situations. They could begin an attack whenever they felt the time was right. In addition, a warrior did not feel obligated to continue a fight simply because his superior wished it. If a warrior grew tired of battle, he could walk away without getting permission from the chief.

White commanders and soldiers often did not understand that Indian chiefs did not have control over their followers. A chief could say that he desired things done a certain way, but his warriors might disagree and do whatever they wanted. The white assumption "that a chief commanded in battle was harmless enough," writes historian Robert Utley. But the assumption "that a chief who signed a treaty or professed peace could bind his people by the pledge caused constant misunderstanding and underlay [caused] more than one war." Since whites wrongly expected an Indian leader who had signed a treaty to be able to enforce it, whites often retaliated against a chief and his village even when these Indians were not the ones who had broken the treaty.

Unfortunately, the peace was broken during the treaty nego-tiations. One of the American soldiers, a New Mexican, saw a horse he claimed had been stolen from him. The soldiers demanded the horse, there was an argument, and shots rang out. As the Indians fled, six Navajos, including Chief Narbona, died. These events happened so fast that the U.S. commanders were not able to stop them.

After this incident, the Navajos were highly suspicious of the Americans. But Calhoun and other officials sent their apologies and insisted that there would be no more such incidents. After a few weeks, Navajo leaders reluctantly agreed to further peace talks. At one meeting, a Navajo chief complained that his people were always asked to return the livestock and other goods they had stolen. But the New Mexicans, he said, never returned stolen goods. "Three of our chiefs now sitting before you," said the chief, "mourn for their children, who have been taken from their homes by the [New] Mexicans. More than 200 of our chil-dren have been carried off and we know not where they are." The Americans insisted that the Indians had initiated the trouble and once more demanded the return of all stolen goods. There was little agreement, and the peace remained uneasy for more than a year.

Increased Tensions and Violence

In 1851, the U.S. Army sought to increase its control over the Navajos by stationing troops on Navajo land. Soldiers erected Fort Defiance in eastern Arizona about thirty-five miles from pres-ent-day Gallup, New Mexico. This was in the middle of Navajo country very near important Indian religious shrines and grazing lands. Thus, to the Indians, the presence of the fort was both an insult and a source of tension. Inevitably, the soldiers and Indi-ans clashed in violent confrontations. In one incident, a Navajo leader turned his horses and cattle out to graze on Indian grazing land. The commander of the fort claimed this was now army grazing land. He ordered a detachment of soldiers to remove the livestock and in the process they shot sixty of the animals. In retaliation, small bands of Navajos attacked isolated groups of settlers. Such violent incidents continued during the 1850s.

By early 1860, the Navajos, angry about increasing numbers of white settlements, stepped up their attacks. The Navajos kept up the fighting, believing that the whites would tire of resisting and leave them alone. The Navajos had never seen more than a few hundred whites in any one place. The Indians had heard stories about white civilization farther east but did not have a clear idea of the real strength of the United States. New Mexican officials, as well as ordinary white citizens, grew increasingly fearful of the Navajo threat. Many officials demanded that the army launch an effective military campaign against the Indians. But the military commander of the region, Col. Thomas T. Fauntleroy, was reluctant to undertake a large expedition against the Navajos. He did not want to start a full-scale Indian war.

The incident that changed Fauntleroy's mind occurred on April 30, 1860. Two Navajo chiefs, Manuelito and Barboncito, led one thousand warriors in a surprise attack on Fort Defiance. Managing to sneak up on the stockade from three directions at once, the Indians streamed through the corrals and buildings of the fort. After driving the white sentries from their posts, the Indians began firing arrows. Some fought the soldiers in hand-to-hand combat. Eventually, however, the soldiers mounted a counterattack and drove off the Indians. Fauntleroy was now convinced that something had to be done about the Navajos.

Chief Manuelito was a fearless warrior who opposed the expansion of whites onto Navajo land.

The Navajo Versus the United States

Fauntleroy put Col. Edward Canby, veteran of the Seminole and Mexican wars, in command of the expedition against the Navajos. Canby recruited eight hundred New Mexicans, some Ute Indian scouts, and five hundred Pueblo Indians, who were enemies of the Navajos, for the campaign. He broke up his small army into several units and ordered them to hunt down and kill as many Navajos as possible. For nearly two months, Canby's forces searched the mountains and deserts of the Southwest for the Navajos. Many of the New Mexicans wore out their horses and almost died of thirst. During the whole expedition, the soldiers managed to kill only thirty-four Navajos. Canby learned that it would be extremely difficult to defeat the Navajos by military means.

Canby returned his army to Fort Defiance. There, in the middle of Navajo grazing lands, he waited. Because of the presence of the soldiers, the Navajos could not return to care for their crops and livestock. Winter was setting in, and there would not be enough provisions to last the season. After several months, some Navajo chiefs, including Manuelito, approached Canby with offers of peace.

Canby, who had become the region's military commander, signed a treaty with the chiefs. The Indians agreed to submit to U.S. authority and to fight the thieves within their own tribe. The chiefs also agreed to move all of their people to the lands west of Fort Fauntleroy. The army had recently erected this fort near Ojo del Oso. In return, Canby agreed to abandon Fort Defiance, which the Navajos had resented for so long. On April 25, 1861, the army withdrew from Fort Defiance and moved to Fort Fauntleroy. In the following months, the Navajos lived in peace with the soldiers. Some Indians and soldiers even participated together in social activities such as horse races.

Indian fighter and well-known scout Kit Carson took charge of hunting down the elusive Navajo.

The Downfall of the Navajos

The peace continued until the army replaced Canby with Col. James Carleton, who had spent time fighting the Apaches in southern New Mexico. Carleton hated all Indians and showed no mercy in his campaigns against them. After defeating one group of Apaches, he created a forty-square-mile reservation for them at Bosque Redondo on the Pecos River in southern New Mexico. This was a remote area with dry, unproductive land. Carleton hoped eventually to send all southwestern Indians, including the Navajos, to Bosque Redondo. There, he believed, it would be easier to watch and control them, and they would no longer be a threat to the whites. Carleton had another reason for wanting to move the Navajos to Bosque Redondo. He was irritated that they occupied some of the richest grazing land in the territory. He believed that this land was wasted on Indians. Sending the Navajos to the reservation would free the land for white ranchers.

At a meeting in Santa Fe, Carleton informed some Navajo chiefs, including Barboncito, that he did not trust them to continue farming and herding in peace. Carleton said there could be peace only if the Navajos moved to Bosque Redondo with the Apaches. Shocked and outraged, Barboncito replied, "I will not go to the Bosque. I will never leave my country, not even if it means that I will be killed." Carleton ignored the chiefs' protests and set a deadline of July 20, 1862, for the Navajos to move. If they refused, he would declare them hostile and hunt them down.

The deadline passed and not a single Navajo had moved. Frustrated, Carleton decided to start rounding up the Navajos and transporting them to the reservation. He changed the name of Fort Fauntleroy to Fort Wingate and made it the base of the operation. He also reopened Fort Defiance, which he renamed Fort Canby. Next, Carleton hired the well-known scout and Indian fighter Kit Carson to take charge of hunting down the Navajos. Carson enlisted some Ute and Apache scouts and led several hundred New Mexican volunteers on a six-month expedition against Navajo villages and lands. The soldiers drove off livestock and burned homes, fields, and orchards. To make sure the campaign was effective, Carleton offered prize money for captured Navajo livestock and bounties for Navajo scalps. The soldiers killed less than eighty of the twelve thousand Navajos, but they virtually destroyed the Navajo way of life. Without their animals, grazing land, and villages, the Indians could not adequately support themselves.

Many of the Navajos retreated to Canyon de Chelly, a large canyon with steep walls and stone dwellings built by earlier Navajos. Here, the earlier Indians had made successful stands against invading Spanish and Mexicans. In January 1864, the soldiers attacked the canyon. They surrounded it, blocked one end, and then moved in with rifles. The troops slowly worked their way through the caves and cliffs where the Navajos were hiding. Most of the Indians had no weapons and resorted to rock throwing to keep the soldiers away. But the Navajos' situation was hopeless. About six thousand Navajos surrendered.

The remaining free Navajos found themselves in equally dire circumstances. Their crops had been destroyed, and their animals taken away. The winter snows came, and there was little to eat. Their Indian enemies, especially the Utes and Pueblos, took advantage of their plight and attacked them. It seemed that there was no other choice but to surrender, and by the end of the year, another four thousand Navajos turned themselves in to white authorities. Only a few hundred Navajos, led by Manuelito, refused to surrender and fled into western Arizona.

A Failed Policy

Carleton proudly reported to Washington that he had ended the problem of Indian raids in the Southwest. And he boasted that he had made rich agricultural and mineral-rich lands available to American settlers. The Navajos, he said, "will have abandoned an area…larger than the state of Ohio to the pastoral [farming] and mining purposes of our citizens."

A Navajo family at Canyon de Chelly in 1873. Whites slowly decimated Navajo populations and strongholds, leaving the tribe splintered and with no way to survive the winter.

James H. Carleton

In the spring of 1862, Col. James Carleton became military commander of the U.S. Southwest. According to people who knew him, Carleton lacked a sense of humor and had a bad temper. He also hated Indians, looking upon them as savages who could not and should not be trusted. Carleton also believed that because Indians often resisted the wishes and orders of the U.S. government, they were enemies of the United States.

Carleton agreed with the U.S. War Department that the best way to deal with the Indian problem was to round up the Indians and put them on reservations. There, they would no longer be a danger to whites. He scouted an area called Bosque Redondo in southern New Mexico on the Pecos River near the Texas border. One reason he chose this as the site of his Indian reservation was that it was far from white towns and settlements.

After the widespread suffering endured by the Navajos at Bosque Redondo, Carleton had to abandon the idea of relocating all southwestern Indians to one area. In 1866, some government leaders said that his policies were too harsh. They forced him to resign his New Mexico command.

Indian Reservations

Reservations are specially designated pieces of land set aside by the U.S. government strictly for use by Indians. It is uncertain who originated the idea, but there were a few reservations already in operation in Virginia, Massachusetts, and other British colonies as early as the mid-1600s. After the establishment of the United States, the American government carried on the tradition of reservations. By 1887, there were over two hundred Indian reservations in the United States covering a total of 138 million acres.

Indians and whites saw the concept and purpose of such reservations very differently. The Indians conceived reservations as integral parts of the treaties they signed with the whites. Between 1778 and 1871 alone there were 389 U.S.-Indian treaties. In each case, the Americans agreed to pay the Indians money and/or supplies in exchange for land. The Indians usually insisted on "reserving" a certain area for themselves, a place where no whites could come. They saw this area as a private domain to practice their religion and customs. Most Indians assumed that they could still hunt on and travel through the lands they had sold.

By contrast, the whites saw reservations as places to confine the Indians. Once a tribe had given up its land in a treaty, the whites believed, the Indians no longer had the rights to use that land in any way. Most whites feared or distrusted Indians and did not want them wandering around in white territories. For the whites, reservations were a convenient way to keep Indians separate from and safely supervised by white society. In most cases, Indians became virtual prisoners on their reservations, unable to travel around the country except with special permission. From about 1820 to 1850, the U.S. government hoped to eliminate the need for new reservations by sending the Indians to Indian Country west of the Mississippi. But as demand for western lands by white settlers increased, the size of Indian Country quickly shrank. The U.S. government once again saw reservations as the only practical solution to the Indian problem.

Shoshone Indians at Fort Washaki, Wyoming Indian Reservation. Some of the Shoshone are dancing as soldiers look on.

But now Carleton faced a problem for which he was unprepared. Thousands of Navajos had to be moved to Bosque Redondo. Both enroute and after reaching their destination, the Indians were totally dependent on the army for everyday necessities. Most of the Navajos lacked food, clothing, and blankets, and the soldiers did not have enough supplies for all the Indians. Before reaching the reservation, many Navajos suffered from exposure, starvation, and dysentery, an infection of the digestive tract. About two hundred of the Indians died on the journey. Even after reaching the Bosque, the Navajos could not fend for themselves. The land was overcrowded and unsuited for agriculture. They had to share the reservation with their traditional enemies, the Apaches, who continually harassed them. The water was filthy, and many Indians became ill from drinking it.

The Navajo situation at Bosque Redondo became so bad that some of the whites in charge of the reservation eventually complained to authorities in Washington. Congress sent a special commission to investigate, and the members of the commission concluded that the Navajos had been treated inhumanely. In 1868, U.S. legislators admitted that the policy of moving the Navajos had failed. They allowed the Navajos to move to another reservation near their traditional home in northwestern New Mexico and northeastern Arizona. Congress had shown more leniency toward the Navajos than it had toward other Indians. But the move did not signal a change in U.S.-Indian policy. Many lawmakers admitted in private that their decision had been based on the knowledge that the Navajos were no longer a military threat. Starving or not, those tribes who still possessed the means to resist the United States received no leniency from Congress. Although conditions on the new reservation were much better than at Bosque Redondo, life for the surviving Navajos remained difficult. Their nation and way of life had been devastated, and most Navajos continue to live in abject poverty.

During more than seventeen years of fighting, the Navajos had earned the respect of many white soldiers. U.S. troops had been surprised at the skill, toughness, and bravery of the Navajo warriors. Yet, another southwestern tribe gave the soldiers far more trouble than the Navajos. During the 1860s and 1870s, the U.S. Army found itself up against some of the most formidable foes it had ever faced. One American general called them the "tigers of the human species." They were the Apaches.

CHAPTER FIVE

The U.S. Government Versus the Apaches

While American troops subdued the Navajos, an even greater threat to white settlers loomed in the nearby deserts. The Apaches had occupied the arid lands of Arizona and other sections of the Southwest for many hundreds of years. There were several different groups of Apaches, among them the Chiricahuas, Mescaleros, Mimbres, Coyoteros, Aravaipas, and Mogollons. There were far fewer Apaches than Navajos. "Altogether, there were probably no more than eight thousand Apaches in the 1850s," says historian Robert Utley. But, emphasizes Utley, "the havoc they created was out of all proportion to their populations."

The Apaches became enemies of nearly all of their neighbors. They continually fought against the Pueblo and Navajo Indians, as well as the Spanish, Mexicans, and eventually the Americans. The reason that the Apaches caused so much trouble was that they often made their livings in an unusual way. The barren desert lands they inhabited were not suitable for farming, so they never became effective farmers like the Navajos. Sometimes the Apaches hunted, but there was little game in the deserts. There were also few edible plants and no grazing lands for livestock. So, when times were hard, many Apaches became thieves, periodically raiding their neighbors for food, horses, and other goods.

Because they were so often at war, the Apaches became formidable fighters. They were experts with the bow and arrow and excellent horsemen. Warriors traveled light. They wore little

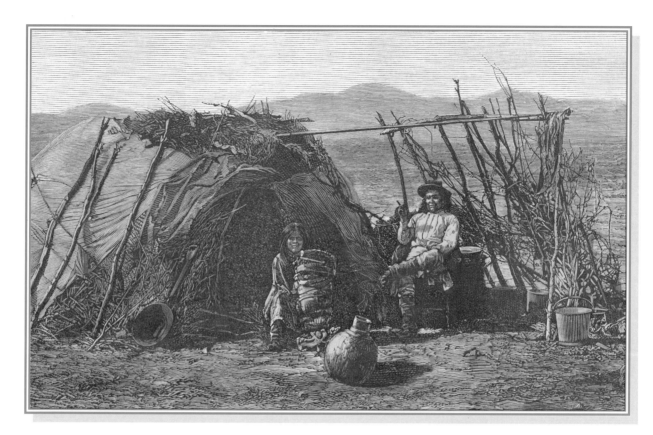

This illustration depicts a typical Apache camp. In the inhospitable deserts that they called home, the Apaches often resorted to thievery for their livelihoods.

more than buckskin moccasins reaching to midthigh and a cloth attached to the waist covering the loins. A buckskin cap with feathers and ammunition belts or quivers of arrows completed the Apache wardrobe. The warriors maintained excellent physical conditioning, enabling them to cover up to seventy miles per day on foot. They also had the ability to hide themselves completely, often appearing to blend into natural surroundings. As a result, American troops often had tremendous difficulty fighting and defeating the Apaches.

Beginning in the 1850s, a major goal of American authorities in the Southwest was to eliminate Apache opposition to whites. The Apaches were a menace to white ranchers and farmers because they raided them so frequently. In addition, important roads leading west toward California passed through Apache country. People and goods moving along these roads also suffered frequent Apache raids. American officials held that the Apaches were dangerous enemies of the United States. U.S. military leaders believed that the best solution was to hunt down the Apaches and force them to live on well-guarded reservations.

Indian Rivalries

The disputes and wars between the Navajos and Apaches were not unusual. American Indian tribes often developed fierce rivalries. Sometimes, as with the Navajos and Apaches, or the Navajos and Pueblos, two tribes were traditional enemies.

Often, however, it was U.S.-Indian policy that created serious rivalries between tribes or even between separate groups within one tribe. This was the case in the Modoc War in northern California and southern Oregon in the 1870s. A band of Modocs under Kintpaush, whom the whites called Captain Jack, lived in a village on Lost River north of Tule Lake in California. Captain Jack asked the U.S. government for a permanent reservation there.

But local whites wanted the land, and the U.S. Army sent cavalry to move the Indians. There was a struggle in which shots were fired and one person from each side died. Captain Jack then retreated with his people to a rough volcanic area called the Lava Beds. There, another Modoc band, led by Hooker Jim, had already taken refuge from the U.S. Army.

The Modoc Indians take up positions against whites after retreating to the Lava Beds.

The two Modoc bands saw the need to unite but disagreed over how to deal with the whites. Captain Jack wanted to negotiate, while Hooker Jim wanted to fight. They took a vote, Hooker Jim won, and the Modocs soon attacked a group of soldiers traveling along an Oregon road. In retaliation, the army sent Edward Canby, veteran of the Navajo wars, with a force of one thousand men against the Modocs. Now, most Modocs wanted to negotiate. However, rivalries between Captain Jack and Hooker Jim continued. Captain Jack met with Canby and afterward received ridicule from Hooker Jim for negotiating rather than attacking the whites. Frustrated and confused, Captain Jack shot Canby in the head during a meeting.

After several battles, Hooker Jim surrendered, and in return for his freedom, helped the soldiers track down Captain Jack. The army hanged Captain Jack, who had originally advocated negotiation. The soldiers then sent Hooker Jim and his people to a reservation.

(Left) The Modoc look out for advancing white soldiers from their stronghold in the Lava Beds. (Below) Captain Jack shoots Gen. Edward Canby during a meeting.

Carleton and the Mescaleros

The Mescaleros, who lived in southern New Mexico, were the first Apache band targeted and defeated by the white soldiers. After raiding settlers in the early 1850s, the Mescaleros fought several skirmishes with American troops. These Indians eventually agreed to stop stealing and tried farming and hunting in the mountains of eastern Arizona. But lack of game and dry soil prevented them from making a living, and they resumed their raids on New Mexican ranches. In 1862, Col. James Carleton, who also opposed the Navajos, launched an expedition against the Mescaleros. His strategy was to hunt the warriors relentlessly and show them no mercy. "The men," said Carleton, "are to be slain whenever and wherever they can be found. Their women and children may be taken prisoner."

Mescalero chief San Juan. The Mescaleros were the first Apache band defeated by the white army.

Under constant pressure from Carleton's troops, the Mescaleros decided to negotiate with the whites. On their way to talks in Santa Fe, however, two of the Mescalero chiefs and their followers were ambushed and killed by soldiers. These troops did not know the Indians were on a peace mission. Despite this unfortunate incident, three other chiefs made it to Santa Fe and met with Carleton. Chief Cadette told the American leader that the Mescaleros wanted peace. The whites had better weapons, the chief said, and the Indians were worn out from running. "We have no provisions," explained Cadette, "no means to live; your troops are everywhere; our springs and water holes are either occupied or overlooked [watched] by your young men. You have driven us from our last and best stronghold, and we have no more heart. Do with us as may seem good to you, but do not forget that we are men and braves." Carleton ordered the Mescaleros to move to the Bosque Redondo reservation in southern New Mexico.

A Spark Igniting War

The army's campaign against the Mescaleros had lasted only about a year. But conflicts with other Apache groups lasted much longer and resulted in much more bloodshed and suffering. When Carleton attacked the Mescaleros in 1862, other Apaches joined forces to oppose the soldiers. Among these were the Chiricahuas, who lived in southeastern Arizona, and the Mimbres, who dwelt in southwestern New Mexico. Their numbers remain uncertain, but there were probably no more than about fifteen hundred warriors in these combined Apache forces.

Each Apache band had serious grievances against whites and other non-Indians dating from years before. The Mimbres' grievances dated back to 1837, when an American trader invited the Mimbres to a feast. At the gathering, the trader suddenly

American Firepower

The possession of effective guns was one of the advantages that helped the Americans gain eventual victory over the Apaches. The Apaches and other Indians sometimes used guns too, but they could not manufacture the weapons. So they usually had access to fewer and less advanced guns than whites did. In a typical frontier battle, only a small percentage of Indians had guns, while every white soldier had one or more.

U.S. soldiers had many types of guns to choose from. One popular weapon was the Colt .45, a six-shooter. A single rotating chamber carried six bullets that shot in succession through the gun's single barrel. Before the six-shooter, pistols had to be reloaded after each shot. Texas Rangers first used the six-shooter in battles against Mexicans and Indians in the 1840s. The weapon also allowed soldiers to fire from their horses. Rifles, by contrast, were designed to be used while the soldiers stood on the ground.

The Americans also had large artillery, including cannons. Standard cannons fired six-, eight-, ten-, and twelve-pound balls. Some cannonballs smashed into and destroyed walls and other structures, while other balls exploded on impact. The howitzer, which could fire shots more rapidly, was an improved version of the cannon.

Another deadly type of American weapon was the Gatling gun, an early version of the machine gun. The Gatling gun had ten barrels that rotated with a crank. If a soldier could turn the handle fast enough, he could fire up to four hundred shots per minute.

Whites had the advantage of superior weapons in their attacks on Indians. (Left) A howitzer was an improvement over other cannons because it could fire more rapidly. (Below) White cavalry carry pistols and rifles as they pursue Indians on horseback.

A Chiricahua Apache family at home. The Chiricahua Apaches and the Mexicans were traditional enemies and often fought one another. After New Mexico became a U.S. territory, however, white soldiers sided against the Apaches in the traditional dispute.

Nana, a Chiricahua sub-chief, photographed in 1886.

opened fire with a large howitzer, killing several hundred Indians. This massacre yielded the trader a bounty of about one hundred dollars per scalp from the Mexicans. At the time, they paid for the scalp of any Apache warrior over the age of fourteen. After this incident, the Mimbres nursed a deep resentment and distrust of whites.

The Chiricahuas had experienced similar troubles. In the summer of 1858, Goyahkla, later called Geronimo, a young Chiricahua leader, led a large group of his people to the Mexican town of Janos. The Indians wanted to trade, pick up rations, and buy whiskey. Leaving the women and children in camp, the men went into town. While they were away, a Mexican commander ordered an attack on the Apache camp. More than 130 women and children died, and another 90 were captured. Geronimo's mother, wife, and three children were among the dead. This incident led to many battles between the Chiricahuas and Mexicans.

Another Chiricahua with grievances against non-Indians was chief Cochise. The war between the Chiricahuas and Mexicans made travel through southern New Mexico unsafe for white Americans during the 1850s. Hoping to avoid war with the United States, Cochise signed a treaty with the Americans allowing a stagecoach station in Apache country. He also agreed to allow white mail carriers to cross Apache territory, promising to protect the mail for a period of three years. He even negotiated a contract to chop firewood for mail employees. Geronimo attended the meetings at which these agreements were made.

But the peace between Cochise and the settlers did not last. An incident in 1861 sparked nearly thirty-five years of war between the Chiricahuas and the United States. A rancher named John Ward wrongfully suspected Cochise of kidnapping his children and stealing his livestock. Ward reported the raid on his ranch to George Bascom, a lieutenant at Fort Buchanan, about forty miles south of Tucson, Arizona. Bascom marched fifty-four soldiers to Apache Pass in the heart of Chiricahua country and asked to speak with Cochise.

At the meeting, Bascom accused Cochise of the kidnapping. The chief protested that he was innocent. He suggested that the Coyotero Apaches may have taken the children, and he offered to help search for them. But Bascom refused Cochise's help and informed him that he was under arrest. The chief swiftly drew a knife, slashed a hole in the tent, and escaped. Bascom then held several members of Cochise's family hostage in order to get the chief to surrender.

These various photographs of Chief Geronimo were taken long after he had ceased to be a formidable enemy of the whites. The woman in the photo at bottom is Geronimo's wife.

Frontier Forts

White soldiers built forts during the history of the settlement of the New World. For more than three hundred years, these structures in the wilderness were the outposts and symbols of the rapidly expanding white civilization. Frontier forts had several purposes, the most obvious being to provide the soldiers protection from Indians and other enemies. Typically, in times of danger, civilians from the countryside surrounding a fort also sought safety within fort walls. Forts could also be used as bases of operation from which to launch offensive military actions. In addition, they served as permanent housing facilities for soldiers assigned to specific regions.

There was little difference in the design of these forts from colonial times until the end of the nineteenth century. Each consisted of a high enclosed wall made of stone or wood, which protected the buildings and people inside. Wooden versions were known as stockades. Sometimes, for extra protection, the soldiers dug a wide ditch called a moat around the stockade. Only occasionally were the moats around North American forts filled with water. Walkways along the top of the outer wall provided positions from which defenders could fire at approaching enemies. Soldiers could also fire through small holes cut in the walls.

Inside the fort were quarters for the base commander and his troops. There was also a jail to hold captured prisoners, a blacksmith shop, and storage facilities for supplies. Most frontier forts had trading posts used by local settlers as well as by soldiers. Thus, these forts often became busy trading and meeting places, attracting people from dozens or even hundreds of miles away. In time, towns grew up around most forts, and some of these towns eventually became important cities. Prominent examples are Fort Detroit in Michigan and Fort Omaha in Nebraska.

Forts were one of the main symbols of white expansion into the west. (Below) An unusual photo of Apache army scouts taken at Fort Wingate in New Mexico. Oftentimes, whites took advantage of Indian rivalries by hiring and training scouts to track down members of enemy tribes. (Bottom, left) Indians approach Fort Union on the Missouri to trade crafts for metal goods and food.

Conflicts in the Southwest

Canyon De Chelly 1864

NAVAJO

Navajo Agency

Ft. Defiance

Ft. Wingate

Prescott • Camp Verde

Santa Fe

Albuquerque • Ft. Bascom

Camp Grant **APACHE**

Bosque Redondo Agency

Tucson

Pinos Altos • Ojo Caliente

Silver City

Bascom Affair 1861

El Paso

Ft. Concho

Areas of conflict in the Southwest

Oregon Country 1846

Mexican Cession after Mexican War 1848

Texas Annexation from Mexico 1845

Louisiana Purchase from France 1803

Red River Basin 1816

Fort

Battles and Sieges

Death of a Chief

Soon, Cochise began raiding the mail routes and capturing hostages to trade for members of his family. Mangas Coloradas, his father-in-law and chief of the Mimbres Apaches, joined in the raids. After the U.S. Army chased the Indians into Mexico, Cochise became convinced that Bascom would never release his family. So the Apaches tortured and killed their hostages. In retaliation, Bascom hanged Cochise's brother and the other male hostages held by the army.

Cochise vowed to fight on, but Mangas Coloradas grew tired of fighting. He watched new U.S. troop reinforcements streaming into the southwestern forts every month and decided that the whites were far too numerous. Fighting them, he reasoned, would be useless and cause the deaths of most of his people. So he and a small band of followers voluntarily surrendered to some white miners. The miners turned the Indians over to local authorities at Fort McLeane in Arizona. There, the fort's commander, Gen. J.R. West, warned the chief not to try to escape. West then told some of his soldiers, "Men, that old murderer has got away from every soldier command and has left a trail of blood for 5,000 miles on the old stage [coach] line. I want him dead or alive tomorrow morning, do you understand, *I want him dead.*" That night, the soldiers heated their bayonets in a fire and sneaked into the tent where the chief was being held. They burned his feet and legs, then shot him four times when he protested. Next, they scalped him, cut off his head, and threw his body into a ditch.

The death of Mangas Coloradas outraged all the Apaches. Geronimo called the murder "the greatest wrong ever done to the Indians." Within two days of Mangas's death, soldiers and Mimbres Apaches fought two skirmishes near Fort McLeane. The soldiers wiped out most of the Mimbres. But other Apache chiefs, including Cochise and Victorio, leader of the Warm Springs Apaches, vowed to drive out the whites or die trying. For two years, Apaches armed with bows and arrows terrorized white settlers in Arizona and New Mexico. With their attacks on travelers, the Apaches made the ninety miles of road between Santa Fe, New Mexico and El Paso, Texas, nearly impassable.

War and Massacre

In the mid-1860s, finding it increasingly difficult to fight the Apaches, U.S. authorities tried to make peace with Cochise, Victorio, and other Apache chiefs. But U.S. commanders said that there could be a truce only if the Indians moved to the Bosque Redondo reservation. The Apaches had heard stories of the starvation and misery suffered by the Mescaleros and Navajos on the reservation. So they refused to negotiate such a deal.

During the next twenty years, the Apaches continued successful guerrilla warfare against settlers and travelers in Arizona and New Mexico. By 1870, Apache raids were a common occurrence. Because he was the best-known chief, Cochise was usually held responsible, although often he was not involved.

Sometimes, U.S. Army commanders tried to make peace with the Apaches but found their efforts sabotaged by local New Mexicans who took the law into their own hands. One such incident occurred after 150 Aravaipa Apaches surrendered to Lt. Royal Whitman in southern Arizona. The Indians handed over their weapons. Whitman then gave them permission to remain on the Aravaipa River near Camp Grant, about fifty-five miles from Tucson, while he awaited official orders from Washington.

In Tucson, meanwhile, a local committee of public safety had organized to protect whites from Apaches. When some Apaches raided settlements near the city, the committee wrongly blamed the Aravaipas camped near Fort Grant. Several hundred angry local volunteers marched to the Aravaipa camp and launched a surprise attack on the Indians. In half an hour, the white vigilantes killed, captured, or chased away every Apache in the camp. More than 140 Indians died, some beaten to death with clubs and stones. The attackers burned the camp and sold twenty-seven children they had taken captive into slavery.

After visiting the ruined Aravaipa camp, Whitman promised justice. He appealed to government leaders, including President Ulysses S. Grant, who expressed outrage over the incident. Thanks to Whitman's efforts, the leaders of the raid went to trial. But the defense claimed that the attackers were justified because they thought the Apaches who raided Tucson had come from the Aravaipa camp. After fifteen minutes of deliberation, the Tucson jury acquitted the men responsible for the Camp Grant massacre. This unfair verdict was not unusual. Other court cases seeking justice for Indians, such as the Cherokee-Supreme Court episode, had ended the same way. Whenever a few sympathetic whites tried to stand up for Indians' rights, the deep-rooted prejudices of the white majority prevailed.

The End of Apache Resistance

For many years, one way the Apaches had eluded capture by U.S. troops was to escape into Mexico. Whites were not allowed to send armed soldiers across the border because it violated the rights of a foreign nation. But in the early 1870s, Gen. George Crook received Mexican permission to cross the border to hunt

A photograph of Geronimo's camp with sentinel standing guard. Geronimo was able to elude capture by crossing the Mexican border when pursued by white soldiers.

Standing Bear's Trial

In most nineteenth century court cases involving Indians, such as the Camp Grant massacre case, the Indians lost. However, there were occasional exceptions, the most famous being the trial of Ponca chief Standing Bear. Like many other Indians, Standing Bear's people had been forced to live in Indian Country. Before removal, their home had been on the Niobrara River in Nebraska. In Indian Country, many of the Poncas died of starvation or exposure, including Standing Bear's son. The leader promised his dying son that he would bury him near his sister, who had died on the Niobrara.

In 1878, Standing Bear and thirty followers set out for the Niobrara carrying his son's body. The band passed many white settlers who had never seen Indians and feared an uprising. So, U.S. troops arrested the Indians near Fort Omaha in Nebraska.

When the army ordered Standing Bear to return to Indian Country, the chief appealed to two prominent American lawyers. They challenged the army's order, saying that the Poncas had rights under the U.S. Constitution. The government's lawyers argued that Indians were not persons under the Constitution. In a decision handed down on May 12, 1879, a Nebraska judge ruled that Indians *were* persons.

Unfortunately, the positive verdict did little to sway the army. Although army leaders allowed Standing Bear to remain in his native Nebraska, they denied him permission to return to the Niobrara. Like the Cherokees, the Poncas learned that a victory in the courts did not mean fair and equal treatment by whites. Despite his win in court, Standing Bear still could not live where he wanted and was not a U.S. citizen. Full citizenship for Indians would not come until the twentieth century.

Chief Standing Bear stares defiantly at the camera. In the U.S. courts, Standing Bear was declared a person under law.

down Indian raiders. Crook's men conducted several exhaustive searches of the mountains in northern Mexico where Apaches, including Cochise, were known to hide.

Unable to find the aging Cochise, Crook sent word to him via an Indian scout promising that the Chiricahua chief would receive respect and fair treatment if he gave himself up. Tired of fighting, sixty-year-old Cochise took this opportunity and surrendered. But once Cochise was in captivity, Crook did not keep his promise. The army placed Cochise on a reservation and made plans to do the same with the rest of his tribe. So Cochise escaped and continued to lead his people against the whites. Later, in September 1872, Gen. Oliver O. Howard approached one of Cochise's camps and asked to negotiate. Howard promised that the Chiricahuas would have a reservation of their own in a place agreeable to Cochise and his followers. Two years later, however, as Cochise lay dying, he discovered that the U.S. government had again broken its promise. To save money, the government decided to place the Chiricahuas on another reservation with other tribes.

An Apache warrior. The Apaches were able to elude the U.S. Army for many years.

General Crook led an exhaustive campaign against the Apaches through extremely rough territory (right). (Below) Faced with the constant fear of white attack, many Apaches surrendered. Here, an Apache chief gives himself up to General Crook.

By 1875, most Apaches were on reservations or living permanently in Mexico. But the Chiricahuas continued to raid parts of Mexico, Arizona, and New Mexico. Throughout the 1870s and well into the 1880s, Geronimo led his people against the U.S. Army. There was public outrage all over the United States that the army was unable to subdue a handful of "savages." Finally, General Crook led five thousand troops, a huge force at the time, in an effort to find Geronimo and his band. After eighteen months of grueling chases and battles in hot desert temperatures, Geronimo finally surrendered.

U.S. authorities now had to decide what to do with Geronimo. President Grover Cleveland considered him a dangerous criminal and wanted him hanged. But other U.S. leaders did not want to make a martyr of the Chiricahua leader. They feared that hanging Geronimo would only anger the Apaches and inspire them to fight on. They persuaded the president to imprison Geronimo instead. Before he died at Fort Sill, Oklahoma, in

Chiricahua Apache prisoners sit on an embankment outside their railroad car in Arizona. Among them is Geronimo (first row, third from right).

Prisoners of the U.S. Army, Apaches sit idle at Fort Bowie in Arizona.

1909, Geronimo became a national celebrity. He appeared at the St. Louis World's Fair in 1904 and in President Theodore Roosevelt's inaugural parade in 1905.

With the capture of Geronimo, the U.S. defeat and relocation of the southwestern tribes was complete. It was now safe for whites to settle the lands on which the Navajos and Apaches had once freely roamed. But the drama of white versus Indian civilizations was not yet over. During the same years that the southwestern Indians fought for their lands, a similar struggle was taking place on the great rolling plains of the American Midwest. Here, the Indians made their last desperate stand against the overwhelming power of the United States.

CHAPTER SIX

Combat on the Great Plains

The Great Plains constituted the last major expanse of unde-veloped territory to be settled by whites. Whites variously referred to this area as the west, midwest, or great American desert. It included most of the rolling prairies stretching westward from the Mississippi River to the Rocky Mountains. Later, this region would encompass the states of Wyoming, Montana, North and South Dakota, Nebraska, Kansas, Oklahoma, and parts of Colorado and Idaho.

In this drawing by Frederic Remington, a Northern Plains Indian warrior slays an enemy Indian on the Great Plains.

To many Americans, the wars against the Indians of the plains symbolized U.S. national progress. By the 1850s and 1860s, nearly all whites accepted the idea that they should settle and develop the west. They believed that building towns, railroads, mines, and ranches would develop and bring civilization to these wild lands. Both the U.S. government and public also believed that a necessary part of progress was eliminating the Indian problem. This meant getting the Indians to live peacefully on reservations and teaching them to adopt "civilized" white ways. If the Indians did not obey U.S. laws, they would have to be pushed aside or eradicated.

The Plains Indians did not understand the notion of progress. They existed the same way their ancestors had, learning to live with nature rather than trying to conquer it. Many tribes, most

White expansion onto the Great Plains (bottom) brought more conflicts with Indians. (Right) An Indian chief prohibits a white wagon train from passing through his country. Such encounters enraged whites, who felt they had a right to the land.

notably the Sioux and Cheyenne, depended on the vast herds of buffalo that roamed the plains for their food, clothing, and other items. The Indians usually killed only the buffalo they needed, so they never depleted the herds and threatened their own way of life. They became seminomadic, following the herds as they migrated. Horses were also important to the Plains Indians. These Indians became some of the greatest riders in history, which also made them very effective fighters. But for all their hunting and fighting skills, the Plains Indians had no chance against the military might of an industrial power like the United States. Thus, they, like other Indians before them, inevitably became victims of American "progress."

Trouble with the Sioux Begins

Some of the Sioux tribes were used to confrontation with whites. Before Europeans landed in North America, several Sioux bands farmed the valleys near the east coast. Decade after decade, the whites pushed them westward. This brought the Sioux into conflict with other Indian tribes. For example, in the early 1700s, they warred with Chippewas in what is now Minnesota. The Chippewas, well armed by French traders, eventually drove the Sioux farther westward and southward into the Great Plains.

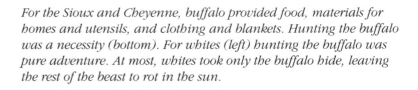

For the Sioux and Cheyenne, buffalo provided food, materials for homes and utensils, and clothing and blankets. Hunting the buffalo was a necessity (bottom). For whites (left) hunting the buffalo was pure adventure. At most, whites took only the buffalo hide, leaving the rest of the beast to rot in the sun.

The Sioux Tribes

The Sioux made up one of the largest of all the American Indian nations. The name "Sioux" is an abbreviation used by whites for Nadouessioux. This was what the Chippewas of Minnesota, their traditional enemies, called them. The two peoples fought each other in the late 1600s and early 1700s until most of the Sioux migrated farther west into the Great Plains. Most Sioux made their living as nomadic hunters, following herds of buffalo and antelope across the prairies.

There were many different Sioux tribes, subtribes, and bands. The Sioux, or Dakota, Nation consisted of seven major tribes: the Mdewakanton, Wahpeton, Wahpekute, Sisseton, Yankton, Yanktonai, and Lakota, also known as Teton.

Each of these tribes had several subtribes. For example, the Lakota, the tribe living farthest west, itself had seven subdivisions. These were: the Oglala, or "Those Who Scatter Their Own"; the Brule, or "Burnt Thighs"; the Miniconjou, or "Those Who Plant by the Stream"; the San Arcs, or "Those Without Bows"; the Oohenonpa, or "Two Kettles"; the Sihasapa, or "Blackfoot"; and the Hunkpapa, or "Those Who Camp by the Entrance." These different groups maintained their unity by attending large tribal meetings every summer. There, they participated in celebrations, exchanged news, traded horses and other goods, and made decisions affecting the entire tribe. Other American Indian tribes had similar subdivisions, although few were as diverse and complex as those of the Sioux.

(Below) A Hunkpapa Sioux warrior, photographed in 1881. (Bottom) A Sioux camp in South Dakota.

By the time of the American Revolution in the 1770s, several large Sioux tribes already roamed the plains hunting buffalo.

Eventually, the expanding United States confronted the Sioux again. The first treaty between the Sioux and Americans was signed in 1851 at Fort Laramie in Wyoming. The United States promised to pay the Sioux in exchange for safe passage for white settlers traveling to Oregon. Other Plains Indians, including the Cheyennes, Arapahos, and Crows, also signed the treaty, which held successfully for three years. Travel for whites seemed so safe that the U.S. Army withdrew some of its regiments from forts in Wyoming and Idaho.

The first serious breach in the peace began in 1854 with an argument over a cow. The animal wandered away from some white settlers traveling along the North Platte River in Wyoming. A Sioux teenager found the cow and butchered it. By the time the cow's owner arrived, several Indians had gathered around to take their share. The owner was afraid to challenge the Indians, so he told the soldiers at Fort Laramie that the Indians had stolen and eaten his cow. A young army officer named John L. Grattan took charge of the case. He had recently graduated from West Point Military Academy and wanted to prove himself to his superiors. Like many Americans, he considered Indians to be ruthless savages who could not be trusted. The incident with the cow seemed to prove this theory.

Grattan marched thirty soldiers armed with heavy artillery to the camp of the Brule Sioux who were protecting the boy who had slaughtered the cow. When the Indians refused to surrender the boy, Grattan ordered his men to open fire with the artillery. The chief of the tribe died in the first volley, and the Sioux warriors swarmed over the soldiers. The troops fled in all directions, but the Indians hunted them down and killed them. A lone survivor reached the fort but died a few days later.

The treaty signing between William T. Sherman and the Sioux at Fort Laramie, Wyoming in 1868. The treaty was broken over a fight about a cow.

Revenge Raid

The incident caused anger and increased tensions among whites and Indians in Wyoming. Outraged over the deaths of their relatives and friends, some of the warriors who had killed Grattan started robbing groups of white travelers along the Oregon road. In the largest robbery, a small band of Sioux held up a stagecoach, killed three men, and took ten thousand dollars in gold. The army then sent Col. William S. Harney to retaliate against the Indians. Harney, a veteran of the Seminole wars in Florida, believed that the Indians should be taught a lesson before any peace talks were held.

In 1855, Harney led several hundred troops in a revenge raid on the Brule Sioux village on Blue Water Creek in Wyoming. After surrounding the village, Harney told Little Thunder, the chief, to surrender the warriors responsible for killing Grattan and robbing settlers. Little Thunder returned to the village. Before he could make up his mind about what to do, Harney attacked. "There was much slaughter," one of the soldiers later recalled. The troops killed about eighty-five Indians and took seventy women and children prisoner. Another one hundred villagers escaped into the countryside. Only four of Harney's men died in the attack.

The attacks by Grattan and Harney on the Blue Water village proved to be seeds that would later grow into a full-scale war on the plains. A young visiting Oglala Sioux named Crazy Horse had witnessed Grattan's senseless attack and bitterly remembered it all his life. Crazy Horse would later become one of the greatest of all Indian guerrilla fighters. The Blue Water incidents convinced him that it was useless to sign treaties with the whites. The only way to deal with the Americans, he told other Indians, was to kill them.

The Sand Creek Massacre

Despite the troubles in Wyoming, many Sioux and other Plains Indians hoped to maintain peace with the Americans. Only a few years later, however, an incident occurred in Colorado that changed their minds. A brutal attack by whites on a Cheyenne village convinced most Indians of the region that Crazy Horse was right. After this attack, which became known as the Sand Creek Massacre, the tribes of the plains began to face the fact that all-out war with the whites was inevitable.

The events leading to the massacre began when gold was discovered near Pikes Peak in Colorado in 1858. Thousands of miners and other settlers rushed into lands that had been guaranteed to the Sioux, Cheyenne, and other tribes by the 1851 Fort Laramie Treaty. American legislators quickly created the

Horses and Warriors

The horse, brought to the New World by the Spanish in the 1500s, transformed the lives of American Indians. "It was as important to him as the coming of steam was to the white man," wrote historian Walker D. Wyman. The horse made the buffalo hunt much more efficient than older hunting methods. These included stalking the animals on foot, driving them into enclosures, burning them in prairie fires, and stampeding them over cliffs. The horse, Wyman speculates, made Indians more mobile, allowing them to follow the buffalo and providing them with more time to fight with other tribes over hunting ranges. In the nineteenth century, mobility on horseback became even more important for Indians. This was because American railroads, wagon trains, and buffalo hunters reduced the amount of game, forcing the Indians to move farther to find food.

Indians clearly excelled in horsemanship. Many nineteenth century observers called them the greatest cavalry in the world. Horses came to be a mark of prestige within an Indian band. A few tribes, such as the Nez Percé in Idaho, became horse breeders. They created a breed called Appaloosas, which have large spots of mixed white and dark brown or black. Explorer Meriwether Lewis described the Appaloosas in 1805. "They appear to be of excellent race," he said, "lofty, elegantly formed, active, and durable."

Many Indian tribes excelled at horsemanship. Here, Indians take cover from bullets by hiding behind their horses.

Colorado Territory, which covered the same area as the present state of Colorado. They realized that most of the Indians would have to move in order to make way for white settlement. So, U.S. officials negotiated a new treaty with the Indians in 1861. The agreement set aside a small section of southeastern Colorado for the Cheyennes and Arapahos. Because this area had little game and was unsuitable for farming, most Cheyenne chiefs refused to sign the treaty. Among the few signers were Black Kettle and White Antelope of the Cheyennes and Little Raven of the Arapahos. They believed that the treaty only specified where their villages must be located. They thought their people still had the right to roam the plains hunting buffalo. This they did all through 1862 and 1863.

Colorado's governor, John Evans, saw the hunters as treaty violators. He claimed that these Indians were trespassing on white lands and, therefore, stood in the way of civilized settlers. He wanted to clear all the Indians from Colorado. Evans appointed Col. John M. Chivington as head of the Colorado militia. Chivington, a former Methodist minister, was described by some who knew him as "a crazy preacher who thinks he is Napoleon Bonaparte." Chivington believed that God wanted him to kill Indians, and he was eager to prove himself a great leader. Evans gave him his chance in a declaration issued on August 11, 1864. The document gave permission to any and all Colorado citizens to attack and kill any Indians they could find, even on lands granted to the Indians by treaty. Evans encouraged the whites "to kill and destroy, as enemies of the country, wherever they may be found, all...Indians." As a reward, whites could keep any property belonging to the Indians they killed.

On November 28, 1864, Chivington marched with seven hundred men and four artillery howitzers into lands occupied by the Cheyenne. The Coloradans immediately closed in on Black Kettle's Cheyenne village on Sand Creek. There were about five

Colorado's governor John Evans wanted to clear all Indians out of Colorado.

This rare illustration shows the Cheyenne camp as the army charges in, gunning down the women and children living there.

Flight of the Nez Percé

The efforts of the U.S. government to seize or reduce the size of Sioux and Cheyenne lands were not isolated cases. This same scenario was repeated many times on the plains. One of the most famous examples was that of the Nez Percé tribe in Idaho, who reacted by trying to escape from the United States. In 1863, the whites imposed a treaty on the Nez Percé that reduced the size of their ten thousand-square-mile reservation to one thousand square miles. This forced them to leave their traditional homeland. The Nez Percé, led by Chief Joseph, fought a number of battles with U.S. troops. Finally, Joseph realized that fighting the whites was futile and, in 1877, he attempted to lead his people to Canada, where the Americans could not touch them.

After a tortuous journey over the Rocky Mountains, the tribe encountered an American stockade in Montana. While Joseph talked with army leaders, his entire tribe sneaked past the white sentries on a mountain trail. This trail was so narrow and dangerous that a soldier later said, "We thought a goat could not pass, much less an entire tribe of Indians." Afterward, the Indians humorously called the stockade "Fort Fizzle" because it had failed to stop them.

Later, about two hundred soldiers attacked the Indians in Montana. Joseph's wife and several other women and children were killed. The tribe's warriors destroyed the American artillery and ammunition, and the soldiers had to retreat. The bitter Chief Joseph later commented, "The Nez Percé never make war on women

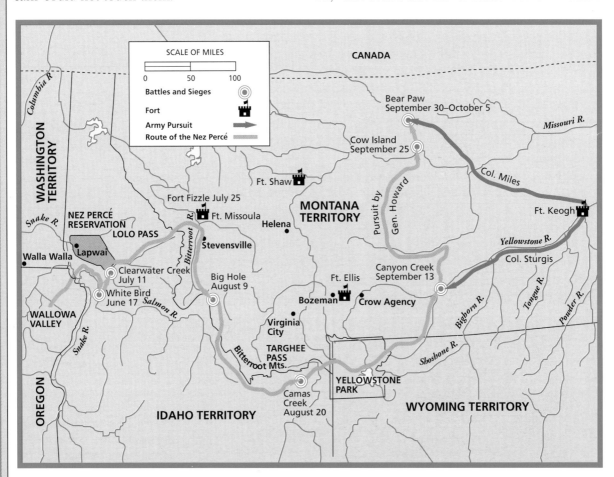

and children; we could have killed a great many [white] women and children while the war lasted, but we would feel ashamed to do so cowardly an act."

Soon after this incident, the Nez Percé passed through Yellowstone National Park, where they captured nine tourists. The army now launched a massive search for Joseph's band. After tricking one U.S. unit with a false trail, the Indians reached the Missouri River on September 23, 1877. A week later, the Nez Percé camped on the Snake River only thirty miles from the Canadian border. Here, about 380 soldiers caught up with them and attacked.

As the troops galloped into the camp, the Indians formed a defensive line and opened fire with guns and bows and arrows. The battle continued off and on until the next day and ended in a stalemate. Twenty-four soldiers had been killed and forty-two wounded. More than a dozen Indians had died in the fight, including Joseph's brother. Joseph himself had been wounded several times and knew that it was useless for his people to go on fighting. When white reinforcements arrived a few hours later, Joseph reluctantly surrendered.

Thus ended the dramatic thirteen-hundred-mile exodus of more than four hundred people who came within only thirty miles of gaining their freedom. In a heart-rending speech on October 5, 1877, Joseph summed up the frustration felt by Indians across the continent about their seemingly endless and futile wars against the whites. "I am tired of fighting," he said. "Our chiefs are killed…. It is cold and we have no blankets. The little children are freezing to death…. Hear me, my chiefs. I am tired; my heart is sick and sad. From where the sun now stands I will fight no more forever."

Conflicts between soldiers and Indians increased after the Civil War. Here, soldiers charge an Indian camp (below). (Right) Nez Percé chief Joseph tried to escape the white army when it became evident that fighting them would be useless.

hundred Indians in the village, most of them women and children. Black Kettle could not understand why the whites would want to attack. He rushed to raise a white flag attached to an American flag. White Antelope, also perplexed, ran toward the soldiers waving his arms and pleading with them not to fire. Suddenly, Chivington ordered his men to open fire, and White Antelope fell dead. The soldiers then poured into the village, firing at every Indian they saw. With cups, plates, even their hands, Indians dug out depressions in the sand trying to create hiding places. But their efforts were useless. One witness later described how the soldiers scalped and cut off body parts of their victims. At least two hundred Cheyennes died in the attack. Black Kettle managed to escape. Having lost only nine men, Chivington returned to a hero's welcome in Denver and displayed one hundred Cheyenne scalps at a local theater.

In 1865, there were both military and congressional investigations into the Sand Creek attack. Both concluded that Chivington was to blame. The congressional committee said that he had shamed his uniform with a "foul and dastardly [cowardly] massacre." But, since by this time Chivington was no longer in the military, he received no punishment. To the whites, Sand Creek was an unfortunate incident. To the Indians of the plains, it was an outrage that would haunt them for generations.

A Policy of Pursuit and Punishment

Angered by the Blue Water and Sand Creek massacres, as well as by white expansion into Indian lands, the Plains Indians began to step up their resistance against the whites. Between 1865 and 1867, the Sioux, Cheyennes, Arapahos, and other tribes regularly raided white outposts and wagon trains. The U.S. Army responded by sending an expedition against the Indians in 1867. Leading the soldiers was Gen. Winfield Hancock. His second in command was a young Civil War hero named George Armstrong Custer. Hancock and Custer chased bands of Cheyennes and Sioux across Colorado, Kansas, and Nebraska all summer. But the warriors always managed to keep ahead of them. Newspapers in the east ridiculed the army's failure to find any Indians. In 1868, Gen. Philip Sheridan, another Civil War veteran, took charge of the operations against the Indians. He vowed to destroy their villages, kill their warriors, and eradicate their way of life.

Meanwhile, Black Kettle approached Gen. William B. Hazen, who commanded the soldiers in Indian Country. Hazen was known to be a fair man who respected the Indians as courageous fighters. Despite the massacre of his people at Sand Creek, Black Kettle said he wanted peace. "I have always done my best to keep my young men quiet," he said, "but some will not listen.

In 1868, Gen. Philip Sheridan took over military operations against the Indians. He vowed to destroy the Indian way of life.

Custer's band leads a surprise attack on Black Kettle's band at Washita. Even though Black Kettle had promised to live in peace with whites, Custer senselessly murdered him and his band.

I have not been able to keep them at home." Hazen was so moved by the chief's sincerity that he offered to protect Black Kettle if war broke out. Hazen was aware of Sheridan's harsh plans for the Indians and worried about what might happen to Black Kettle. But the chief said he should remain with his people, who were now camped along the Washita River in Oklahoma. Hazen promised that Black Kettle and his people would be safe on the Washita for the winter.

Only weeks later, trouble arose between Hazen and Custer. They had known each other at West Point and had never gotten along. Custer disagreed with Hazen that Black Kettle posed no threat. Custer agreed with Sheridan that the Indians must be pursued relentlessly, punished, and forced into submission. Hazen argued that negotiation was a better course, but Custer would not listen. After leaving Hazen, he prepared his men for an attack.

On the morning of November 7, 1868, Custer led a surprise attack on Black Kettle's village. Most of the warriors were away on a hunt, and the village was inhabited mainly by women and children. With his band playing, Custer charged his Seventh Cavalry into the village and the soldiers began killing. Black Kettle put his wife on a horse and tried to lead her to safety. But a column of soldiers shot them down and galloped over their bodies. The soldiers killed about 140 Indians and took several dozen prisoners. They also took the village's winter food supply so that any survivors would face starvation.

In the following few years, Custer and his colleagues continued their policy of pursuit against the Indians. In response, many Cheyennes, Sioux, and other tribes began to band together. In a heroic attempt to defend their homelands, they would win a stunning victory that would be remembered for all time. That same victory would mark the beginning of the end of their way of life.

CHAPTER SEVEN

Defeat

By the early 1870s, a few thousand Indians blocked total U.S. control of the lands stretching from ocean to ocean. The Sioux, Cheyenne, and a few other tribes in Montana, Wyoming, and South Dakota believed that if they stood united, they could stop the whites. Acting together, they staged a daring, courageous, but ultimately hopeless attempt to save the last great Indian frontier.

In their dealings with the Plains Indians, whites were driven by the same anti-Indian prejudices that had existed since the 1600s. To whites, Indians posed a threat to decent, civilized Americans who wanted to build homes and raise families on the plains. Whites believed these lands belonged to the United

Miners pan for gold in Colorado in 1859. In addition to the desire for more land, white settlers' search for gold led to the displacement of Indian tribes.

States. In addition, railroad and mining companies wanted to exploit these lands.

This determination to own Indian lands was reflected in the new western military leaders in the 1860s. Many of the commanders who took charge of the western forts, like Sheridan and Custer, were veterans of the recently ended Civil War. So were many of the enlisted men. That incredibly bloody conflict had left many of these men hardened to the sight of cruelty and bloodshed. To these soldiers, the Indians were a clear threat to the country. This view shaped the U.S.-Indian policy laid out by General Sheridan in the late 1860s. The U.S. War Department had assigned him the task of bringing the Plains Indians under control. The government had given him permission to handle the situation in any way he saw fit. The Indians, Sheridan stated, were dangerous enemies of the United States. They would be treated as such. Custer's merciless destruction of Black Kettle's village on the Washita in 1868 set the tone for the U.S. assault on the remaining Plains Indians.

War Parties Sweep the Plains

Following the Washita massacre, the Sioux and Cheyennes stepped up their raids on white travelers and settlers. With the Blue Water and Sand Creek tragedies still fresh in mind, many tribes united. This growing alliance included several bands of Sioux, including the Oglala Tetons under Red Cloud and Crazy Horse and the Hunkpapa under Sitting Bull. Joining them were northern Cheyennes under Chief Dull Knife and the northern Arapahos under Chief Black Bear. War parties from these bands raided ranches and attacked American soldiers. They soon brought American traffic moving west almost to a standstill.

Following the Washita massacre, Great Plains Indians retaliated by attacking whites moving west, such as this wagon train in 1879.

One reason the Indian war parties were so effective was that Red Cloud and Crazy Horse had developed a new type of battle strategy. Part of this strategy involved a decoy-and-attack maneuver. Crazy Horse and a few warriors would ride into full view of the U.S. cavalry. The Indians would then act surprised and run away. The soldiers, believing they had the upper hand, usually followed, only to be ambushed by a waiting group of Sioux. In one incident, Crazy Horse, acting as a decoy, lured eighty soldiers under Capt. William Fetterman to their deaths. After the soldiers followed Crazy Horse, more than fifteen hundred Sioux surrounded and annihilated them.

Crazy Horse introduced other battle innovations. He introduced battle plans in which each warrior played a specific part. He knew that the U.S. Army operated this way and that it was one of the reasons for their success. He brought battlefield discipline to Indian warriors, and this made them even more effective fighters than before. Crazy Horse and Red Cloud taught others to use these same techniques.

After white soldiers began stepping up their attacks on the Indians, including massacring their women and children, Indian bands began to form an alliance to fight the whites. Included in this alliance were the Hunkpapa tribe under Chief Sitting Bull (left) and the Oglala Tetons under Crazy Horse (right). The photograph of Crazy Horse cannot be verified. It is not known whether Crazy Horse was ever photographed.

Red Cloud

ed Cloud was a chief of the Oglala Teton Sioux. He steadfastly refused to allow whites to build roads across his land near the Powder River in Montana. But the U.S. government sponsored the building of a road anyway and erected two forts to protect it. When the Plains Indians rose up against the whites in the late 1860s, Red Cloud led the Oglalas against whites attempting to use the road. For more than two years, the Indians made it nearly impossible for whites to travel through the area.

White authorities eventually offered to negotiate with Red Cloud about the road. The two sides signed a treaty at Fort Laramie in Wyoming, in 1868. Under the treaty, the government promised the Sioux the western half of South Dakota and agreed to abandon the road through Red Cloud's country. Red Cloud later burned the forts that had guarded the trail.

Years later, when the soldiers forced the Sioux onto reservations, government authorities tried to undermine Red Cloud's authority so that he would not lead any Indian uprisings. But Red Cloud remained a powerful influence on his people. He showed his contempt for whites by refusing to sign a treaty in 1889 that broke up the largest Sioux reservation. Late in life, he became a Roman Catholic. Although he did not believe in the Ghost Dance religion that swept the plains in 1890, he sympathized with its followers. Red Cloud died in 1909 at the age of seventy-seven.

Oglala Sioux chief Red Cloud.

The Dispute over the Black Hills

The continuing problems and hatreds between Indians and whites eventually peaked over the issue of the Black Hills. Many Plains Indians, including the Sioux, considered these forested mountains in South Dakota to be sacred land. Many Indian cemeteries were located there, and the Indians believed the spirits of their ancestors roamed the hills. Former treaties between the Indians and the Americans had guaranteed that no whites would ever be allowed to enter the Black Hills.

Blatantly ignoring these agreements, Custer, with Sheridan's approval, led an expedition into the hills in 1874. Some western settlers had pressured the government to explore the hills for possible gold deposits. So, the expedition included an engineer, a geologist, a botanist, and other scientists to study the land. They were accompanied by a massive military assembly: more than one thousand cavalry, two hundred foot soldiers, 120 wagons, and three large artillery pieces. The expedition encountered no Indians. But newspaper reports following the expedition's return blared in large headlines that there was gold in the Black Hills. In 1875, tens of thousands of prospectors, settlers, and adventurers poured into the sacred lands.

To the Sioux and other Plains tribes, the violation of the Black Hills was the greatest outrage yet perpetrated by the whites. In the winter of 1875, bands from many tribes came together in southern Montana near the Little Bighorn River. They met to plan strategy to take back the Black Hills as well as to hunt in one of the few hunting grounds still unguarded by the whites. Thousands of Indians, perhaps the greatest number ever to assemble in one place, gathered in a village that covered several square miles.

A huge column of cavalry, artillery, and wagons makes up the 1874 expedition into the Black Hills led by Custer.

George Armstrong Custer

Born in New Rumley, Ohio, in 1839, Custer attended the United States Military Academy at West Point. He graduated last in his class in 1861. In addition to being only an average student, he lacked discipline and often broke the rules. Nevertheless, Custer had a magnetic personality, tremendous confidence in himself, and easily inspired others to follow him. After graduating, he received an immediate assignment in the Civil War and fought in the First Battle of Bull Run.

Custer quickly showed himself to be a brilliant, though often impetuous, cavalry officer. He became famous for leading daring cavalry charges against the enemy even when the odds were overwhelmingly against him. Luckily for Custer, all of these charges were successful, earning him a number of rapid promotions in rank.

During the Civil War, Gen. George A. Custer was known as an impetuous and daring leader.

Custer loved the feeling of power that came with commanding armies and ordering men into danger. He saw himself as a larger-than-life hero and attempted to project a dashing, colorful, and unique image. He grew his sandy blond hair to shoulder length and donned specially made uniforms covered with medals and gold trim. His unusual appearance and reputation for battlefield heroics made him famous to both Union and Confederate soldiers.

After the war, in 1866, Custer became a lieutenant colonel in the Seventh Cavalry in Kansas. There, he took part in expeditions against the Indians. Like many other Americans, Custer considered Indians inferior to whites and felt that they stood in the way of white progress. Custer agreed with his commander and friend Philip Sheridan, whose comment—"The only good Indian that I ever saw was dead"—became famous. In November 1868, Custer attacked and massacred a group of Cheyenne Indians camped on the Washita River. This and other such wanton attacks earned him the praise of many whites and the hatred of the Plains tribes.

The Indians finally got their revenge on the man they called "Yellow Hair" in 1876. Commanding only 675 men, Custer approached a vastly superior force of Indians who were camped on the Little Bighorn River in Montana. He divided his forces into three groups, his own numbering just 267 men. By the time he realized that the Indians numbered in the thousands, it was too late. Combined forces of Sioux, Cheyennes, Arapahos, and other Indians closed in and surrounded Custer. He and his entire command were wiped out in what became the most famous Indian battle in history. A young Arapaho warrior who fought in the battle witnessed Custer's death and later described it to a historian many years later:

He [Custer] was dressed in buckskin, coat and pants, and was on his hands and knees. He had been shot through the side, and there was blood coming from his mouth. He seemed to be watching the Indians moving around him. Four soldiers were sitting up around him, but they were all badly wounded. All the other soldiers were down [dead]. Then the Indians closed in around him and I did not see any more.

Curley was Custer's Crow scout at Little Bighorn.

The Last Great Indian Victory

The U.S. War Department knew that the white invasion of the Black Hills would anger the Indians and increase the danger of attacks on settlers. The department also knew that the Indians were gathering in Montana. War Department officials issued a warning to all Plains Indians in 1875. If by the end of the year the tribes were not on specific reservations that had been designated for them earlier, they would be hunted down and dealt with in the harshest terms. The Indians may not have received this warning, but if they did, they ignored it. Their great camp in Montana continued to expand.

When the Indians did not move, the U.S. Army began planning a major spring offensive against the Montana Indian camp. It was a three-pronged attack. One group of soldiers, led by Gen. George Crook, marched north from Fort Kearny in Wyoming. Another group under Col. John Gibbon marched from western Montana. The third group consisted of the Seventh Cavalry commanded by Alfred Terry and George Custer. Their orders were to march west from Fort Lincoln in the Dakota Territory. The plan was for the three groups to converge on and destroy the Indian camp.

Custer and the other army leaders were confident of victory. They had nearly two thousand troops altogether, and they expected to meet a force of no more than fifteen hundred Indians. What they did not know was that the camp on the Little Bighorn already held more than seven thousand Indians.

Custer was the first commander to reach the vicinity of the Indian camp. Eager for action, he led about 675 men ahead of

(Below, right) General Crook and his troops at camp.

Terry's column and reached the Little Bighorn on June 24, 1876. His orders were to wait for Terry, Gibbon, and Crook to arrive. But Custer, who had a history of disobeying orders, thirsted for the glory that would come from defeating the Indians on his own. The next morning, having no idea of the enemy's strength, he prepared to attack. He divided his men into three units, one commanded by Capt. Frederick Benteen and another led by Maj. Marcus Reno. Custer took charge of the third group, which consisted of 267 men. Custer ordered Reno to move along the south side of the river, then attack. Custer would ride around the village and attacked on the opposite end.

Late that morning, with about 280 men, Reno approached the lower end of the village and attacked as ordered. He met with fierce resistance from Sitting Bull's Hunkpapas. As hundreds of warriors charged, Reno's men held their ground for about ten minutes. The air was filled with dust and smoke, and the gunfire and war screams of the Indians were deafening. Reno became confused, first ordering his men to dismount, then ordering them to mount again. A bullet hit his scout in the head, splattering the brains on Reno's face. As the Indians drove his men back, he ordered a retreat to a hill across the river. While his men dug into the hill to set up a defensive line, Benteen's detachment of 125 men arrived. Reno's and Benteen's combined forces desperately

Capt. Frederick Benteen (top, left), Maj. Marcus A. Reno (top, right), Gen. Alfred Terry (center), and Gen. George Armstrong Custer (bottom, right) were part of the force that was to attack the Indians gathering at Little Bighorn.

held off the Indian onslaught. After a while, fewer and fewer Indians attacked the hill. Something seemed to be drawing them away.

Reno and Benteen did not realize that most of the warriors in the village were now converging on Custer's command in the rolling hills on the other side of the river. No one knows why Custer became surrounded. According to the later testimony of Indians who fought in the battle, the Indians sighted Custer's group just after Reno retreated across the river. The Cheyennes under Lame White Man and the Hunkpapas under Gall rushed toward the rear of Custer's troops. At the same time, Crazy Horse's Oglalas attacked the soldiers head on. Thousands of Indians took part in the bloody assault, during which most of the soldiers dismounted and separated into small groups. Here, Crazy Horse's new battlefield strategy worked brilliantly. The Indians attacked in well-coordinated waves, overwhelming the troops. In the space of about forty-five minutes, Custer and all of his men were killed. The only Seventh Cavalry survivor of the battle was a horse named Comanche.

In both of these illustrations of Custer's last stand, a beleaguered Custer and his men face off against Indians on all sides.

Eventually, Terry, Gibbon, and the other reinforcements arrived and found Reno's and Benteen's tattered units still holding the hill near the village. By this time, the Indians, aware that more soldiers were approaching, had moved away. Terry and Gibbon also found the remains of the slaughtered Seventh Cavalry. The Indians, following their normal custom, had stripped the bodies of boots and most clothing. Partly from custom and partly for revenge, they had also used knives to mutilate many of the corpses. The soldiers found pools of dried blood near Custer's head. After the battle, some Cheyenne women had recognized Custer, whom the Indians called "Yellow Hair" and "Son of the Morning Star." The women punctured his eardrums with long needles several times. Years before, the Cheyennes had warned Custer that if he continued to attack the Indians, he would die. He had not listened. Now, the women tried to clear out his ears so that he would hear better in the afterlife.

The grisly remains of Custer's last stand (right). (Below) The white markers above the graves of Custer and his men are erected on the battlefield where they fell.

Indian Land Cessions

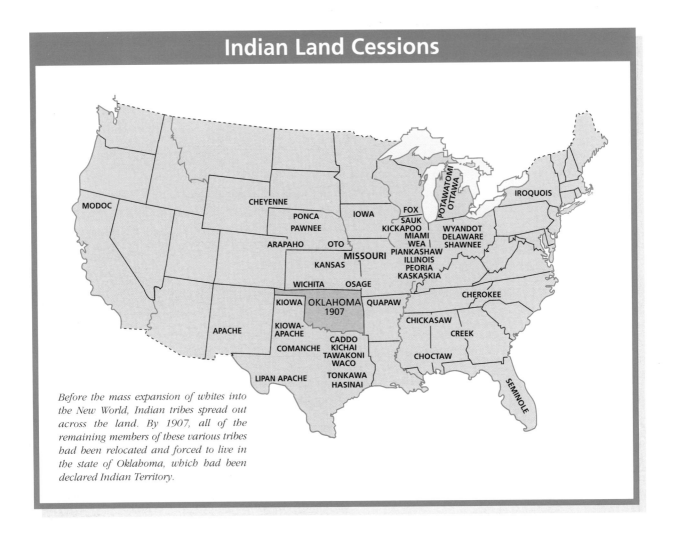

Before the mass expansion of whites into the New World, Indian tribes spread out across the land. By 1907, all of the remaining members of these various tribes had been relocated and forced to live in the state of Oklahoma, which had been declared Indian Territory.

Downfall of the Sioux Nation

The U.S. War Department responded to the Custer defeat by heavily reinforcing western forts. Within weeks, twenty-five hundred additional soldiers joined Terry's and Crook's armies, and the government began building more forts in Montana and Wyoming. Crook and other commanders chased the Sioux, who had made the mistake of splitting up into small groups after the Little Bighorn battle. Sitting Bull and his band escaped into Canada, while Crazy Horse and the Oglala fled southward.

For months, the soldiers pursued Crazy Horse and his people, giving them little time to rest. Finally, in May 1877, Crazy Horse surrendered. He had not been defeated, but his people had grown weary of fighting and running. "I want this peace to last forever," Crazy Horse said as the soldiers led the Oglalas toward a reservation.

U.S. Army commanders worried that Crazy Horse, who had become a hero to all Indians, might still be a threat. The

Cheyenne Autumn

After Custer's defeat on the Little Bighorn River in 1876, the U.S. public called for revenge against the Indians. Responding to this call, Gen. George Crook and Col. Nelson A. Miles led a major campaign against the Cheyennes during the winter of 1876-1877. After the soldiers defeated the Indians in a number of battles, the Cheyennes, led by Dull Knife, surrendered. They expected to go to the Sioux reservation near their traditional hunting grounds. But the army sent them to Indian Country instead.

The Cheyenne found life in Indian Country unbearable. The land was impossible to farm, and the government failed to furnish the supplies it had promised. In addition, the Indians caught diseases from the whites, and many Cheyenne children died. Dull Knife and his people finally decided to sneak away and attempt to return to their homeland. On September 9, 1877, about three hundred Cheyenne quietly headed north. They crossed fifteen hundred miles of plains on which many whites had settled. More than ten thousand soldiers and three thousand white civilians chased the band northward. The Indians became trapped and subsequently escaped several times. Finally, the soldiers caught up with them. When the army said that they had to go back to Indian Country, some of the Cheyennes tried to run away. During the bloody roundup that followed, more than one hundred Indians died. Eventually, the government granted Dull Knife's band a small patch of land in Montana. But, by that time, only eighty members of the band were still alive.

When Cheyenne chief Dull Knife surrendered, he and the remainder of his tribe expected to go to the Sioux reservation. Instead, they were sent to Indian Country where many of the tribe suffered and died.

commanders feared he would stir up trouble on the reservation or escape and lead another uprising. So, in September, General Crook ordered his men to go to the reservation and arrest Crazy Horse. The Indian leader would be shipped to a prison in Omaha, Nebraska, where he could no longer influence his followers. So that he would not know he was being arrested and try to escape, the soldiers invited Crazy Horse to army headquarters to talk. When the soldiers began escorting him to the guard house, he realized he had been tricked. As he desperately struggled to get away, they stabbed him. They then carried him to an office where he died that night.

After the death of Crazy Horse, the army continued to round up Sioux and other Plains Indians and force them onto reservations. The government also continually reduced the size of the reservations in order to make more land available for white settlers. Soldiers watched the Indians carefully and did not allow them to travel off the reservations without armed escorts.

The Dance of Salvation

Arapaho Indians perform the Ghost Dance. Adherents of the Ghost Dance believed the Indians would magically triumph over whites.

Fearing their civilization was nearing extinction, many Indians desperately resorted to a new religious belief that promised the salvation of their race. Called the Ghost Dance, it became popular

on most of the Plains reservations in 1890. Like Christianity and other religions, the new faith promised life after death. But the Ghost Dance also predicted that, through magical powers, the Indians would drive the whites off Indian lands. The whites would be pushed back into the great sea from which they originally came. The Sioux wore special shirts for the Ghost Dance ceremony. These shirts, believers said, would make them immune to the white soldiers' bullets.

Army commanders and government officials feared that the Ghost Dance would lead to more Indian uprisings. So, soldiers began arresting the Ghost Dance leaders. Some of those who practiced the faith fled into the Badlands, a desolate area of South Dakota. Cavalry units gave chase and killed several of the Ghost Dancers. The survivors took refuge with Chief Big Foot's Minniconjou Sioux on the Cheyenne River reservation. Now, the army believed, Big Foot was a threat.

On December 28, 1890, the cavalry surrounded Big Foot and his people and marched them to Wounded Knee Creek in South Dakota. They planned to disarm the Indians and ship them to an

(Above, right) Minniconjou Sioux chief Big Foot allowed Ghost Dance leaders to take refuge with his tribe. (Below) Big Foot's band on the Cheyenne River Reservation. Almost all of these Indians were killed at the Battle of Wounded Knee.

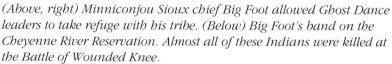

Omaha prison. The next morning, during the disarming process, an Indian protested. As the soldiers tried to seize his weapon, it accidentally went off. Instantly, the troops began a killing spree, firing away at unarmed men, women, and children. Big Foot, who was suffering from pneumonia, helplessly watched the massacre until he too was killed. When it was over, 153 Indians lay dead.

The incident at Wounded Knee was the final armed clash of the Indian Wars. When the whites began settling America in the 1600s, there were more than two million Indians living in what is now the United States. In 1890, fewer than 250,000 Indians inhabited these same lands.

During all these years of war, the white position had remained the same. It held that a superior civilization had the natural right to take the lands of an inferior civilization. Many Indians, by contrast, held that the Creator had made the land

After the Battle of Wounded Knee, Chief Big Foot lies dead and frozen on the snow-covered battlefield (left). (Below) Men gather the frozen corpses of the dead.

A group of Sioux Indian warriors in war dress.

without boundaries. Therefore, people had no business trying to divide or own the land. The great Nez Percé leader Chief Joseph had said, "I see the whites all over the country gaining wealth, and see their desire to give us lands which are worthless.... Perhaps you [the whites] think the Creator sent you here to dispose of us as you see fit.... The one who has the right to dispose [of people and land] is the one who has created it. I claim a right to live on my land, and accord you the privilege to live on yours." But Joseph's offer of mutual respect was rejected. The white position prevailed.

The Struggle Continues

The story of the American Indian did not end at Wounded Knee. White civilization had destroyed much of the traditional Indian way of life, such as subsistence hunting and nomadic life-styles. But many tribes continued to attempt to hold onto their traditions on government-sponsored reservations. By the early 1920s, there were 285 federal and state reservations, most of them located west of the Mississippi River. After the end of the Indian Wars, Indian populations began to rise for the first time in hundreds of years. In 1890, there were about 250,000 Indians in the United States. By 1960, that number had grown to 509,000. The 1990 census counted more than 1,400,000 Indians in the United States.

According to historian Carl Waldman, in the late nineteenth century, the official goal for Indians was self-sufficiency, "But it was self-sufficiency through terms dictated by whites—i.e., the suppression of Indian culture and the adoption by Indians of white traditions and technologies." To achieve this assimilation, the U.S. government implemented a policy called allotment.

In 1887, Congress passed the General Allotment Act, under which Indian reservations were broken up and allotted in 160-acre parcels to heads of Indian families. The government thought that making responsible individuals owners of the land would allow the land to be developed and farmed more quickly. When the Indians did not use the land as Congress had envisioned, it passed other legislation that allowed the leasing of Indian land to whites. The allotment policy further worsened Indian conditions by decreasing tribal landholdings. During the allotment period, which ended in 1921, Indians lost millions of acres of land—nearly two-thirds of what they were originally allotted in 1887.

Another way government encouraged assimilation was by passing laws to discourage cultural differences. Legislation of the period made it illegal for Indians to wear their hair long and also outlawed rituals such as the Plains Indian Sun Dance. Federally run boarding schools attempted to teach Indian children white ways. There were almost no schools on reservations.

As the twentieth century began, Indians still had no rights under American law. They were not citizens and could not vote. They could not own land or operate businesses in white communities. They could not travel around the country without special permission and remained virtual prisoners on their reservations.

In this sentimental portrait of a Navajo Indian mother and child taken from a newspaper Sunday magazine, the artist underplays their Indian features, making them look like whites. When Indians were no longer a threat to white civilization, popular culture romanticized their culture.

A Glimmer of Understanding

After the Indians ceased to be a threat to whites, however, some of these policies began to change. After many Indians fought in World War I, whites became a bit more sensitive to conditions on the reservations. White government investigators found living conditions on these reservations poor. There was little food, and few Indians had jobs, schooling, or medical care. In 1921, Congress passed the Snyder Act. This redefined the duties of the Bureau of Indian Affairs. This agency of the U.S. Interior Department had been created in 1824 to help formulate government policies regarding Indians. Its position had reflected the general attitude of white society, that Indians should assimilate into white culture. Now, under the Snyder Act, the bureau was ordered to help improve living conditions on the reservations and teach the Indians new irrigation and farming methods.

In 1924, Congress passed the Indian Citizenship Act, which gave U.S. citizenship to all Indians born in the country. Indians could now leave the reservations and travel wherever they wished. They could also vote in local, state, and federal elections. Indians had finally become citizens of an area they had

Indians are taught blacksmithing at an Indian training school in Oregon. Indians were encouraged to abandon traditional ways and assimilate into white culture.

occupied for centuries. The only exception was in Arizona and New Mexico, where whites continued to block Indian voting rights. (After winning cases in court in 1948, however, Indians won the right to vote in these states as well.)

In 1934, under the leadership of President Franklin D. Roosevelt, Congress passed the Indian Reorganization Act. Called the Indian "New Deal" by many historians, the act eliminated the policies of assimilation and allotment, protected tribal landholdings, and returned some lands originally allotted. In addition, the act encouraged tribal constitutions and courts, business corporations, and education by providing federal monies and loans to tribes for these purposes.

President Franklin Delano Roosevelt passed the Indian Reorganization Act. The act promised to be an Indian New Deal.

Encouraging Assimilation

As in the past, U.S. government policy did not remain consistent, however. In the 1950s, many of Roosevelt's Indian programs came under attack. New government leaders returned to encouraging Indian assimilation and discouraging Indian cultural differences. Many officials also recommended less government monies be devoted to Indian affairs. These new policies had both bad and good effects. In 1952, Congress established the Voluntary Relocation Program. The program offered counseling and financial assistance to Indians who wished to relocate off reservations. The government offered help in finding new residence and employment. While this policy did improve conditions for many individuals, it also resulted in a "brain drain" as the most promising individuals left the reservations to become integrated in white society. In addition to this policy, from 1954 to 1962, the government stopped sponsoring social, educational, and health services and facilities for sixty-one Indian tribes, bands, and communities. Unfortunately, without government sponsorship, many of these communities sank deeply into poverty. Congress responded by reestablishing its involvement with some Indian tribes who suffered under the new policy. Eventually, the government abandoned attempts to cease involvement in Indian affairs and went back to subsidizing reservations.

Reclamation

While Congress struggled with how to deal with Indians on the reservations, it also struggled with Indians who wanted to reclaim lands taken from them during the centuries of the Indian Wars. In 1946, in response to these demands, Congress made it legal for Indians to sue the government for claims involving land the United States had taken illegally during the Indian Wars. By 1967, the Indians had won $208 million in 101 cases. During

Members of AIM occupy Alcatraz Island in an effort to gain support and sympathy for the living conditions of American Indians.

Chief Homer St. Francis of the Abenaki tribe holds a favorite picture of a Native American trapped behind the bars of a flag. St. Francis and other Abenaki are protesting the building of a dam near their reservation in Northeastern Vermont because they fear it will damage ancestral burials, hunting, and fishing grounds.

these proceedings, much proof came to light about the way the government had cheated the Indians in the 1800s. Although Indians have been successful in some of these cases, the success has been muted by criticism. Many argue that the monies paid to the Indians were worth far less than if the Indians had actually received payments in land.

Indians succeeded in having actual lands returned in only a few cases. In 1971, for example, the government agreed to return forty-eight thousand acres of the Blue Wilderness Area in New Mexico to the Taos Pueblo. In 1972, the government returned twenty-one thousand acres to the Yakima tribe in Washington.

Although official government policy is to allow Indians more self-determination in their own affairs, many problems still exist for the Indians. Living conditions on the reservations are still much worse than in the rest of the country. As Carl Waldman notes in *Atlas of the North American Indian,* "On a national average, Native Americans have the shortest life span of any ethnic group; the highest infant mortality rate; the highest suicide rate; the lowest per capita income; the highest unemployment rate; the highest high school dropout rate; the poorest housing, and the most inadequate health care, with extensive diabetes, tuberculosis, high blood pressure, respiratory disease, and alcoholism." According to *The Final Report of the American Indian Policy Review Commission,* published in 1977, alcohol abuse was "the most severe and widespread health problem among Indians today." Nationally, the report found, around half of the adult American Indian population is chemically dependent to some degree.

On reservations across the nation, Native Americans fight for land rights. Here, Jeff Sohappy (left), a member of the Yakima tribe, talks with reporters in Oregon after receiving a citation for using a dipnet to fish. Dipnets are illegal in Oregon, but are a traditional method of fishing for the Yakima.

Indian Protest

In the 1960s and 1970s, a number of college-educated members of the Indian community formed organizations and rights groups to protest conditions on the reservations. One of the most important is the American Indian Movement (AIM), founded in 1968 in Minneapolis. In 1969, members of AIM occupied Alcatraz Island and gained worldwide attention and support for their efforts. Another dramatic protest, called the "Trail of Broken Treaties," occurred in 1972, when Indian rights activists occupied the offices of the Bureau of Indian Affairs in Washington, D.C. A year later, a group of Indians and whites seized the village of Wounded Knee, South Dakota, in order to call attention to Indian problems. Indian activists continue to fight the U.S. government to gain recognition and economic reparation.

Today, a resurgence of interest in Indian life-styles and cultures has occurred throughout the United States. Many people across the country attend Indian tribal events in national parks and on reservations. Kevin Costner's popular film *Dances with Wolves* (1990) did much to foster a national interest in Indians' plight and culture. But in spite of this renewed sensitivity, for most Native Americans, a lot of work remains to be done. They continue to fight for the restoration of sacred lands from the U.S. government, sacred relics and objects from U.S. museums, and for political and legal recognition. The legacy of the Indian Wars lives on.

For Further Reading

Dee Brown, *Bury My Heart at Wounded Knee*. New York: Holt, Rinehart & Winston, 1970.

Benjamin Capps, *The Indians*. New York: Time-Life Books, 1973.

Frederick Drimmer, ed., *Captured by the Indians: 15 Firsthand Accounts, 1750-1870*. New York: Dover Publications, Inc., 1961.

Jason Hook, *American Indian Warrior Chiefs: Tecumseh, Crazy Horse, Chief Joseph, Geronimo*. Dorset, U.K.: Firebird Books, 1990.

Alvin M. Josephy, Jr., *The "Patriot Chiefs"*. New York: The Viking Press, 1961.

David Nevin, *The Soldiers*. New York: Time-Life Books, 1973.

Francis Paul Prucha, *The Sword of the Republic: The United States Army on the Frontier, 1783–1846*. Bloomington: Indiana University Press, 1977.

Robert M. Utley, *Frontier Regulars: The United States Army and the Indian, 1866–1890*. New York: Macmillan, 1973.

Robert M. Utley, *Frontiersmen in Blue: The United States Army and the Indian, 1848–1865*. New York: Macmillan, 1967.

Robert M. Utley and Wilcomb E. Washburn, *Indian Wars*. Boston: The American Heritage Library of Houghton Mifflin Company, 1987.

Robert M. Utley, *The Last Days of the Sioux Nation*. New Haven: Yale University Press, 1963.

Carl Waldman, *Atlas of the North American Indian*. New York: Facts on File Publications, 1985.

Works Consulted

John W. Bailey, *Pacifying the Plains: General Alfred Terry and the Decline of the Sioux, 1866–1890*. Westport, CN: Greenwood Press, 1979.

John S. Bowman, ed., *The World Almanac of the American West*. New York: Ballantine Books, 1987.

Richard Drinnon, *Facing West: The Metaphysics of Indian-Hating and Empire-Building*. Minneapolis: University of Minnesota Press, 1980.

Francis Jennings, *The Invasion of America: Indians, Colonialism, and the Cant of Conquest*. New York: W.W. Norton & Company, Inc., 1976.

Alvin M. Josephy, Jr., *The Indian Heritage of America*. New York: Alfred A. Knopf, 1970.

Michael Paul Rogin, *Fathers & Children: Andrew Jackson and the Subjugation of the American Indian*. New York: Vintage Books, 1976.

Thomas Henry Tibbles, *Buckskin & Blanket Days*. Lincoln: University of Nebraska Press, 1969.

Herman J. Viola, *After Columbus: The Smithsonian Chronicle of the North American Indians*. New York: Orion Books, 1990.

John William Ward, ed., *Webster's Guide to American History*. Springfield, MA: G. & C. Merriam Company, 1971.

Index

Photo Credits

Cover photo by Library of Congress

AP/Wide World Photos, 120 (top)

The Bettmann Archive, 24, 40, 50, 68

Colorado Historical Society, 95 (top)

Kirk Condyles/Impact Visuals, 120 (bottom)

Custer Battlefield National Monument, 107 (all)

The Daughters of the Republic of Texas Library, 51 (both)

Denver Public Library, Western History Department, 12 (both), 63 (bottom), 95 (bottom), 97 (bottom), 99

C.S. Fly/Courtesy Museum of New Mexico, 83

Illinois State Historical Library, 88, 113 (bottom)

Bette Lee/Impact Visuals, 121

Library of Congress, 10, 11, 13, 14, 16, 17 (both), 19, 20 (both), 21, 28, 29, 30 (both), 31 (all), 32, 35 (both), 38 (both), 39, 42, 43, 47, 49 (bottom left), 52, 53, 57 (both), 61, 74, 75 (bottom), 77 (bottom), 79 (middle and left), 86 (top), 89 (both), 90 (both), 94, 100, 105, 108 (both), 109 (bottom), 119

Minnesota Historical Society, 115

National Archives, 15, 46, 49 (top, bottom right), 55, 63 (top), 67, 69, 70, 76, 78 (bottom), 79 (right), 80 (right), 86 (bottom), 87, 91 (both), 92, 97 (top), 98, 101, 102 (left), 103, 104, 106 (all), 109 (top), 111, 112, 113 (top), 114 (top), 118

The National Portrait Gallery, Smithsonian Institution, 33, 37

Nebraska State Historical Society, 114 (bottom)

Prints Old & Rare, 22, 64, 73, 75 (top), 77 (top), 78 (top), 85 (all), 117

South Dakota State Historical Society, 84, 102 (right)

The Thomas Gilcrease Institute of American History and Art, 80 (left)

Woolaroc Museum, 59 (both), 60

About the Author

Don Nardo is an actor, film director, and composer, as well as an award-winning writer. As an actor, he has appeared in more than fifty stage productions. He has also worked before or behind the camera in twenty films. Several of his musical compositions, including a young person's version of *The War of the Worlds* and the oratorio *Richard III*, have been played by regional orchestras. Mr. Nardo's writing credits include short stories, articles, and more than twenty-five books. Among his other writings are an episode of ABC's "Spenser: For Hire" and numerous screenplays. Mr. Nardo lives with his wife Christine on Cape Cod, Massachusetts.